HEREFORD
R. Lugg
R. Frome
Castle Frome
Stoke Edith
Mordiford
MARCLE HILL
R. Wye
Ross
Goodrich Castle
MONMOUTH
LEDBURY
Much Marcle
Mathon
Bosbury
Eastnor
MALVERN HILLS
GREAT MALVERN
Malvern Wells
Little Malvern
Leigh
Bransford
Castlemorton
Birtsmorton
Pendock
R. Leadon
NEWENT
May Hill
Mitcheldean
Westbury on Severn
GLOUCESTER
Corse
Ashleworth
Tirley
Hill End Court
UPTON ON SEVERN
Earl's Croome
Pirton
Besford
Croome Court
PERSHORE
R. Avon
Defford
Eckington
Woolas Hall
Strensham Court
Ripple
Bredon
Twyning
TEWKESBURY
Deerhurst
Tredington
R. Severn
BREDON HILL
Overbury
Bickford
Toddington
Elmley Castle
Netherton
Cropthorne
Fladbury
Charlton
Harrington
Abberton
Lench
Abbott's Salford
Bidford
Grafton
R. Avon
Middle Littleton
EVESHAM
Wickhamford
R. Isbourne
Stanway
Didbrook
Winchcomb
Sudeley Castle
Southam Delabere
CHELTENHAM
COTSWOLDS

198

Hear hills do lift their heads |
aloft from whence sweet |
springes doe flow :
Whose moistvr good doth |
firtil make the valleis |
covchte belowe.
Hear goodly orchards |
planted are in frvite |
which doe abovnde
Thine ey wolde make their |
hart rejoyce to see |
so plesant grovnde !

*—On a Sixteenth-Century Sheldon
tapestry map woven by Richard
Hyckes of the Shires of Worcester
and Warwick. Now in the
Bodleian Library.*

PREFACE

THIS book is written to please, and has not for its existence the usual rough pragmatical excuse of an area-book —that people can use it to find their way about. It is full of unessential information, and might once have been indicted on this score. But this very uselessness has now the full approval of the law, in that the publication of " local guide-books " has become a criminal offence; what might have seemed an indefensible farrago must now be considered a model of warlike discretion. An Englishman outside his own county is made to feel an invader : routeless in a forbidden land, he must calculate his position by the sun. The excitement of travel, which is not a quality of countries for which a visa must be sought, but an attitude of mind, may now be learnt at home.

Nevertheless, the foundation of an area-book still lies in picking and choosing among previous authors, and I should be ashamed to enumerate all those from whom I have taken what here passes as my own. Mention is made in the text of Mr. R. C. Gaut and Mr. G. C. Allen, and it is a pleasure to remember Mr. P. B. Chatwin's survey of Warwickshire Monuments, Mr. Oliver Baker's Shakespearian studies, and the work of the Royal Commission for Historical Monuments in Herefordshire. I am also indebted to Mr. R. Ironside for innumerable suggestive comments and a phrase about Burne-Jones ; I have been privileged to consult Mrs. K. A. Esdaile upon one point ; Mr. Lawrence Gowing has awakened me to certain elements in John Guldo, and I have envied Mr. Peter Ramsbotham his feeling for brasses; Miss Esther Darlington has introduced me to the song of Ivor Gurney with which the book ends. I am grateful also for the extreme kindness with which we were received, often at moments inopportune to themselves, by many owners and guardians of property, and particularly by Lady Vernon, Lord Cobham, Lord Doverdale, and Mr. Edmonds of Croome Court. Miss Prudence Willoughby has been kind enough to help me with the proofs. But my heaviest debt and most patent obligation is to my publisher, Mr. Harry Batsford, and the fact that this is the experience of all his authors does not make it less pleasant to record.

J. R.

97 CHEYNE WALK, LONDON, S.W.10
December 1941

ACKNOWLEDGMENT

THE Publishers must express their thanks to the following photographers for contributing illustrations : Aerofilms Ltd., Fig. 86; the Architectural Press, Fig. 116; the British Council (for photos by J. Dixon Scott, F.R.P.S.), Figs 20, 21, 23, 26, 27, 28, 32, 38, 111, and 118; E. J. Burrows Ltd., Cheltenham (photos by Stanford & Mann Ltd., Birmingham), Figs. 45, 46; Eric Cheshire, Fig. 93; the late Brian C. Clayton, Figs. 9, 54, 63, 64, 101 (1-4); Country Life Ltd., Figs. 5, 66, 70, 77; the Rev. F. Davenport, Rector of Strensham, Fig. 4; Herbert Felton, F.R.P.S., Figs. 47, 110, 117, 125; Mrs. Paul Foley, Fig. 142; Fox Photos Ltd., Figs. 113, 143; F. Frith & Co. Ltd., Reigate, Figs. 37, 65; Ewing Galloway, New York, Fig. 43; Miss Frances Hope, Fig. 19; A. R. Kersting, F.R.P.S., Figs. 18, 101 (5), 107; Brendan Kierney, Worcester, Fig. 135; Keystone Press Agency, Fig. 112; Dorien Leigh Ltd., Figs, 8, 31, 69, 80, 96, 115, 133; Midland Air Services Ltd., Fig. 52; Sydney Pitcher, F.R.P.S., Gloucester, Figs. 6, 7, 97, 98, 108, 130; John H. Stone, Figs. 3, 14, 35, 36, 39, 49, 78, 102, 132, 136; Will F. Taylor, Reigate, Figs. 12, 15, 22, 24, 25, 29, 40, 41, 48, 60, 81, 85, 91, 94, 95, 123, 128; Tilley & Son, Ledbury, Fig. 103; Miss M. Wight, Figs, 2, 30, 53, 55; F. R. Winstone, A.R.P.S., Figs. 13, 16, 58, 59, 89, 131.

With regard to drawings, the following must be thanked: the British Museum, Fig. 44; the Bodleian Library, Oxford, Fig. 73; Mr. W. A. Forsyth, F.R.I.B.A., Figs. 11, 100, 140; Mr. W. Curtis Green, R.A., Figs. 18A, 57, 68, 71-2; Mr. Sydney R. Jones, Figs, 51, 56, 79, 121. Fig. 33 is from the late Oliver Baker's *Shakespeare's Warwickshire*, by kind permission of Mrs. Baker; the endpaper maps have been drawn specially by Miss Norah Davenport, who has also redrawn other subjects. It is unnecessary for reviewers to enlarge on their inadequacy; in a work of this type large-scale coloured maps are always entirely impracticable. These are at least of some use for reference, and for detailed study standard larger-scale maps are still readily available.

For coloured plates, the frontispiece is by Mr. Illingworth Varley, whose decease during its reproduction is deplored; Fig. 120 is by Mr. Sydney R. Jones and Fig. 62 is by Mr. A. Troyte Griffiths, architect, Malvern, who also died suddenly during the production of this book. The blocks for it have been kindly lent by Messrs. Newman of Tewkesbury. The lines by Ivor Gurney, with which the book ends, are included by arrangement with his publishers, Messrs. Sidgwick & Jackson Ltd. They appear in his *Songs from Severn and Somme*.

CONTENTS

2 WILD DAFFODILS ON THE HILLS ABOVE STOKE EDITH

3　THE FLATTENED DOME OF MAY HILL : A dominant point above Newent

I

INTRODUCTION

THERE used, at Creil, to be a taxi-driver whose special talent was the "tour Nervallien." That is to say that anyone accepting his offer would be taken, beneath the immigrant skies of the Ile de France, as far as can be covered between lunch and dinner, being ceaselessly informed the while of those incidents in de Nerval of which the landscape at that instant on view might well have been the setting. Thus at one moment Sylvie, at another the Filles du Feu, sometimes even the whole of La Bohème Galante, were brought before the customer, and this landscape-with-commentary was the best of entertainments, leaving to the imagination neither too little nor too much. Yet to reproduce it on paper, and between covers, would be difficult, and raises the whole problem of the country-book.

The country-book is a curious genre, bought on impulse or at Christmas, commonly making little stir in the mind. Successful country-books are praised mostly for their illustrations ; these, one hears, are what people want, and only the most neurotic, habit-ridden reader, able to feast off the backs of railway-tickets or the by-laws of a fallen republic, can claim to have read the text of a country-book. Writers, moreover, on a particular area seem subject to an inertia not found among those writing generally of country life ; Mr. Bates and Miss Sackville-West, for example, have the same themes as Vergil and Theocritus, and yet do very well ; whereas the area-book, in which almost everyone could newly illuminate his subject, is seen very often to languish. This is due in part to the strange sexual-anthropomorphic idiom of English country-writers, in which villages nestle,

A

valleys girdle, and rivers are said to have issue ; illumination ceases with the first of these tropes, leaving not so much as a candle. Also, these writers have no formal criteria, such as occur immediately to writers on more specialised subjects, and thus fall back on beauty, which everyone knows to be a most awkward concept, known by many names, and a bad traveller. Yet the possibility of error, so readily admitted in the humanities, is usually no element in the country-book ; this, we hear, is beautiful, and was short-listed for the British Council calendar ; this, unhappily, is not. It is, in short, very puzzling to see what sort of people must write country-books ; and yet it cannot be entirely a black market, for some excellent work has been done in it, and before beginning I took pains to find out how this was.

With books on defined aspects of the country, on church furniture or the cottage or the elimination of wire-worm, it is of course another affair. These are exact, minute, and learned subjects, open to critical estimate ; each is a vocation, and if Mrs. Esdaile's subject were not one's own, one would still read reviews of it, as of Finer on Constitutions or Onions on Elizabethan diction. The trouble about the area-book is that, while it may treat ambulando of many learned subjects, it has never itself been the object of formal stricture, or had to go before the tribunal which the overwhelming increase in empirical knowledge has set up for every other kind of book. It should be taken for granted of the author of a new area-book that he is an economic geographer, a sociologist, an æsthetic and political historian, profoundly interested in people and a natural, easy writer ; instead, the area-book is the last refuge in literature of the personal extravaganza, an enchanting genre, but one which is not here in place.

Any reader has the right, in return for the credits of good-will which he advances in beginning a book, to make certain demands of the author—that he will respect, for example, the challenge of Blake. " I will not cease," said Blake, " from mental fight " ; and any book of whose making this is true will show in all its lineament the marks of hard, combative thinking. It will not, like most country-books, be about a strange, sub-Miniver world in which people " espouse " causes, are " keen about " religion, marry " good ladies," a world in which one does not see two monuments, but rather " accepts an invitation to meet a stately couple from Stuart England."

5 GEORGIAN GOTHIC, CROOME

4 MEDIEVAL STRENSHAM

CONTRASTING CHURCH NEIGHBOURS WITH THEIR CROWDED MONUMENTS

6 MONUMENT TO THE LATER FRANCIS RUSSELL,
STRENSHAM CHURCH

There is, moreover, a new significance in the goodness of a good book on the country, a new shame in the badness of a bad one ; for the war has a two-way grip upon authors, at once deterring—as paper is short and authors who are not very good authors are better employed away from their desks—and encouraging, for people now need particularly to read about the country of which each of us is newly aware. Moreover there is a new impermanence about the country-writer's subject. Stone is become as fugitive as fountains' water. Now that the air above our capital is no longer bent in the manifold signature of Wren, we look with special appeal to the country, finding a new assurance in each apparent sign of English living. That is why the man to write an area-book just now will not be one native to the country, but one bred to the generalised amenity of urban life and coming upon the area by the accident of war, an exile before the unhelpful dispersion of country life, seeing the area, not with the golden-wedding tenderness of the local writer, but with impatient, if delighted, analysis. Two of the best of recent country-books, for example, have been by John Piper and Paul Nash, who are not properly either writers or country-men ; and I wonder to what extent our daily preoccupation with the progress of the war will have fitted us each to seize upon the significance of an unfamiliar area.

This view has, moreover, the authority of precedent. Consider the two foremost of Worcestershire historians— Habington and Nash. Of these, Thomas Habington (1560– 1647), a graduate of Lincoln College, Oxford, and a student at Rouen and Paris, godson of Queen Elizabeth, son-in-law of Lord Morley, was nevertheless just such a peppery, ingenious old type as we shall find to be common in Shakespeare's country ; an unquenchable Papist, he spent six years in the Tower for his activities in support of Mary Queen of Scots, and only on being forbidden to leave his native county did he decide to become its antiquary ; nor was he cured of plotting and contriving, but made of his house at Hindlip a veritable warren of secret holes, in one of which the Jesuit Henry Garnett was captured in 1605. Nash, by contrast, took up the country-book as a counter-temptation to " elections, gaming, horse-racing, fox-hunting, and such other pleasures as are the ruin of country-gentlemen." Nash was of a gentler, more apprehensive cast than Habington ; born in 1725, he went to Worcester College, Oxford, and married one of the Overbury Martins ; he was rector successively of Leigh (1792) and Strensham (1797). At Leigh he is said to have lived in luxury, and at Strensham the rectory, remote from any other habitation and buried in a laurel forest of a depth found usually only at boarding-schools, survives unchanged to-day. A man of calculation and foresight, he became son-in-law to Lord Somers and annually, on the Sunday preceding the audit of tithes, preached on the text, " Owe no man anything." In 1793 he published an edition of *Hudibras* (its author a native of Strensham), which is of interest in that it had engravings commissioned from Hogarth.

Here then are these two distinguished original country-writers—the fathers, one might say, of their profession ; one took to the work as an exile from London, the other to offset the otherwise invincible attraction of pleasure. Nothing could more exactly define the conditions in which I took up this work, and all hesitation was instantly banished. This area seems to me to have no rival candidate. We want an area well provided by nature but yet (since the survey must hearten us for our immediate task) entirely adapted to man, displaying all his skill. It must have been a successful area in industry and commerce, so that ambitious citizens will have stayed at home, enriching their neighbourhood by the decent splendour of their homes, the endowment of churches and civic buildings, and the patronage, for their funeral monument, of the best of living artists. Not so successful, however, as to have devastated its natural aspect, subjected its population to the hazard of commercial fluctuation, and exterminated indigenous crafts. It must have been near enough to London to have been, until the Restoration, a centre of political consciousness ; yet not so near as to have been consumed in the later extension of the capital. It must, in fine, combine the energy and acumen of the north with the discretion and tranquillity of the south. Thus the courtesan counties, Devon, Cornwall, and the Lakes, are excluded, as of natural rather than social interest ; the North Midlands also, as a subject mainly of social controversy ; the East and South, because the recent history of the English mind in society could be written with only passing reference to them. There remains the heart of England, richly gifted by nature and an object of human effort since the first civilising attempts of the overrunning

Romans. Like the great gorse-brake of which Coleridge
spoke, it has long stood in the sun, throwing out its pods in
every direction of human activity. In agriculture, the breeding
of domestic beasts, private and official architecture and
decoration, in fishing, sculpture, political science and the
amalgamation of industry it has made itself a national symbol.
Ideas, as strenuously as armies, have fought upon its soil.
It heard the first enunciation of those ideals of liberty which
are our present charge ; and it is associated with one whom
many think the greatest of Englishmen—it is Shakespeare's
country.

Shakespeare's country is a large, irregular, fertile, watery
plain, including Warwickshire, Worcestershire, and contiguous parts of Herefordshire and Gloucestershire. It is
bounded by the Cotswolds, the Malverns, and the industrial
massif to the North. It contains two man-size and traffic-
laden rivers, the Severn and Avon, and many smaller ones,
the Stour and Teme and Lugg, together with canals. It is
naturally well wooded, and was additionally afforested by
Henry II. ; it retains, for example, a forest of seven acres
near Bewdley. It is a fruiterer's paradise, and the vale of
Evesham in blossom is lovely as Sparta silver with olives.
Geologically it is freakish, and the Malverns often ring with
the flute-like barking of amateurs of this subject ; but it has
also those solid veins of iron and coal which made possible
the early and economical encouragement of indigenous
industry, when the Restoration had diverted the nimblest
wits from politics to commerce. The profusion of wild
flowers (of which 7000 varieties are found near Bredon) is
itself an epitome of the generous natural provision of the
area.

Yet it is the human resources which are the glory of
Shakespeare's country. Other areas have their fine beasts,
rivers bursting with salmon, trout, grayling, and eel, their
seams of mineral, deep woods, and long acres of busy soil.
Other areas are more amply picturesque. But none has such
splendour of persons. None has so consistently formed the
national taste and reflected the national temper. No other
part has so often stood for the whole. The history of the
area is one of commercial success, decisive political activity,
and enlightened patronage. The whole integument of life
displays the wise use of ample profits and the splendid fury

of conscience in action. The great tithe barns of Worcestershire witness to the acumen of those religious houses to
whom, before the Dissolution, so much of the county belonged.
Such beautiful towns as Painswick (this, however, is strictly
outside the area) are eloquent of the enlightened wealth of
the wool-trade ; and even such plain market-towns as Stratford were fat with trade and, if not ravaged by fire or flood,
can still show fine examples of Tudor building. Nor was
it only the ruling class who lived becomingly ; the magpie
half-timbered cottage of this area (8, 9, 128) is too familiar
to need description, while in later times the model village
designed by Feargus O'Connor at Staunton displays the
early working of social conscience. The nose for a deal, so
natural to this area, is shown by the readiness with which
timber was sacrificed to feed the new furnaces of industry ;
and it was in the eighteenth century, when the highly evolved
political sense of this people had no longer outlet in action,
that its enterprise was fully apparent.

Characteristically this was preceded and accompanied by
a great burst of lovely and original building. To the great
castles of Kenilworth (10), Maxstoke (53), and Warwick (78),
the great family homes of Westwood (62, 71), and Charlecote (17), and Compton Winyates (61), were added new
marvels ; first there were local architects of great talent
(e.g. Thomas White, a pupil of Wren, who between 1702–05
built the Guildhall and the churches of SS. Nicholas and
Swithin and All Saints at Worcester (18) ; or Sanderson
Miller, who later in the century built Warwick City Hall,
Radway Grange, and restored Kineton Church) ; and in
addition the area could attract the most distinguished of
contemporary architects and decorators. Even before the
Civil War there were presages (at Aston Hall, for instance)
of the new division of functions, and with the Restoration
the employment and separate contract of individual artists
became common. Few great houses did not take part in the
war, and many were damaged or wholly destroyed, for this
was a running war, and isolated houses, as well as three-
quarters of Birmingham, were constantly burnt or razed or
penetrated by single balls. Thus new building was everywhere encouraged, and many estates, whether from lack of
heir or the necessity of realising capital, changed hands, and
this was made the occasion of experiment. Thus this area

7 THE AVON BY BREDON HILL with Bredon spire

8 IN INKBERROW, WORCESTERSHIRE

9 NORTON BY EVESHAM

is an excellent playground for anyone with an anti-antiquarian bias, for circumstances have everywhere favoured the ordered elaboration of the late seventeenth and eighteenth centuries, at the cost of the fortified manor and the maniacal rambling burrows of Tudor times. By many of these examples, as by the work of Sir Henry Wotton in his *Elements of Architecture* (published shortly before the outbreak of Civil War), we are reminded that this is Descartes' century, a time when the

10 KENILWORTH CASTLE IN THE EIGHTEENTH CENTURY

discovery of method profitably curbed the free exuberance of the Renaissance ; and it is instructive to compare the adaptations of more recent times with such cases as that of Enville House, an Elizabethan banqueting house, to which four wings were added in 1660, or, still better, of Westwood (62, 71) ; nothing so distinguishes a living architectural tradition from a dead one as a comparison between the amendments made to Westwood at the Restoration, and those, relatively small in extent but ruthless in effect, of the present century. A few years later it was possible for anyone, at no very great expense, to enjoy such a product of civilisation as survives at Hagley (69, 70) or Hanbury (65, 66). To this period belong, moreover, such refinements as the shallow-relief plasterwork introduced by Italian stuccatore; and the landscape garden, the pastime equally of poets and prime ministers, developed that subjection of nature which had begun with the topiary and was to end with the pinetum.

It is no coincidence that this period of invention, of Highnam, Combe, and Compton Verney, was also the period of the Lunar Club at Birmingham. This club was an intellectual centre of Athenian brilliance; it was as if all the passion and energy, all the striving and dialectic of the Civil

[*Drawn by W. A. Forsyth, F.R.I.B.A.*

11   EARLY TUDOR GABLES, TEWKESBURY

War had been suddenly turned to the advance of science and the development of industry. Boulton, Watt, Wyatt, Murdock, Priestley, Erasmus Darwin, James Keir, Dr. Withering, Parr the Greek scholar, Baskerville, and Wedgwood between them gave to man the discoveries of oxygen and digitalin, advances in botany, physics, and chemistry, ecclesiastical history, printing, humane letters, and the production of china,

12 WELFORD-ON-AVON, WARWICKSHIRE

13   THE LEICESTER HOSPITAL, WARWICK

14   THE "BLACK BEAR," TEWKESBURY

TIMBER TUDOR WORK IN TOWNS

such as no group has since been able to show. Unhappily the area was not ready for such initiative, and in 1791 rioters destroyed the homes and papers of many of the members, so that Birmingham became known more for commercial achievement than for any mastery of absolute problems. The growth of this city, and, later, the new educational systems of Arnold at Rugby and the Hills at Edgbaston, display ideally the transposition of those qualities of thoroughness and invention, of response to new conditions, which have always characterised the area. By the late nineteenth it had already, through its largest town, regained political eminence, and its leading family of Chamberlain was become as influential as the Cecils.

This great initiative neither evaporated the industries native to the area, nor hindered its free architectural development. Indeed its exemplary balance of heavy and service industries (typified by the happy adoption, at the turn of the century, of the motor-car and cigarette industries) has maintained the area in decent prosperity even during the slump of the last decade.

During the Regency, the area profited by the ravages of colonial life to the extent of acquiring one of its most beautiful towns; for it was found that the magnesian waters of Cheltenham, patronised in 1788 by George III., were specially soothing to systems burnt out by long residence in the tropics. This happy chance caused to arise, between 1810–30, the most delicate and harmonious town in England—one remarkable less for individual buildings (for these might often singly appear insipid) than for the constant small perfection by which the eye is met (19, 116–8). This town is a personal, perhaps even a constitutional, taste; to coast through its crescents, promenade, and acacia-shaded avenues is to hear an old, thin, bony music, as if someone in an empty house were to play, upon a wooden-framed piano, a sonata of Weber.

Cheltenham apart, the area is still rich in nineteenth-century curiosa. Many leading revivalists chose, like Gambier Parry, to live in it, and from the architects who ornamented the new opulence of the South Midland manufacturer a whole Gothic alphabet could be made, beginning with Ashpitel, Barry, Blomfield, Bodley, Dawkes, Fowler, and Gibson. The Grecian, the Italianate, the French Château, the German with

B

Ionic portico, the Houses of Parliament—no expression of this imitative age is missing. Teulon, Rickman, Nesfield, windows by Clayton and Bell, restoration by Scott, and frescoes by Parry, the gamut is run again and again.

It might seem that all this is headlong windy stuff, with nothing to do with Shakespeare. Yet the stuff of Shakespeare, in so far as we can apply it to our own work, is the invention, the unexpected use of existing means, the turning about. All of this seems to me to sit in with the personal history of this part of England; and to pick up even a quarter of it, the explorer must go unexpectedly armed, like that Venetian conspirator who never went abroad "but with a pistol concealed in 's cod-piece." I pick up Shakespeare, as it seems to me, when I come by road to Tewkesbury and see the Abbey tower swing like a great Stilton across the eye's field, or in reading of Edward II.'s death, and the solitary hawk wheeling above Berkeley; or in the many fine testaments of the Civil War; or in the indifference to popular hatred of Priestley and Murdock. This is a general concept, leading perhaps away from Shakespeare rather than towards him; going towards him, it is necessary to remember that Shakespeare is wrought in so closely with the English character that only a foreign observer can truly assess the difficulty of this task. Delacroix, for example, says of him: "Les Anglais sont tout Shakespeare; il les a presque faits tout ce qu'ils sont en tout." The greatness of an author is measurable by the number of angles from which it is possible to make a useful entrance into his work, and anyone writing now on Shakespeare is likely to be misled, for instance, by the view of Walter Raleigh, for this, enthroned in the celebrations of 1916, has now general credence. Philistinism has no subtler weapon than this—the challenge to renounce kinship with "Cromwell, Milton, Chatham, and Johnson" sooner than with "Drake and Sidney, Bacon and Raleigh." Not simply is this a false opposition, wrongly aligning the parties of both groups, but it establishes a tie-up, not only between Shakespeare and the sixteenth century, but between the sixteenth century and all right-thinking readers. This is cant, for not only is it in the seventeenth century that England established the type of post-Renaissance democracy, but the whole climate of the previous century was one in which its champions would instantly have perished. Shakespeare was in no sense a

15 CRADLEY, NEAR MALVERN

16 AT WELFORD-ON-AVON

17 CHARLECOTE HOUSE BY THE AVON

18 ALL SAINTS CHURCH, WORCESTER

conformist author, and we shall best be able to read him if
we seek out those characteristics in his country which, if
general, would perpetuate the strenuous element defined by
Coleridge when he said, "Shakespeare lived in an age in
which, from the religious controversies, carried on in a way
of which we have no conception, there was a general energy
of thinking, and an expectation of it in those who came
forward to solicit public praise, of which, in this day, we are
entirely ignorant." It is in this that Shakespeare anticipates
the seventeenth century, in which even such a baby-face
as Cowley could dispute with Hobbes, attend courses of
physics in Paris, draw up schemes for colleges of agriculture
at Oxford and Cambridge, be himself an expert botanist, and
embody, in fine, within his own curly, pouting head, something of the arduous temper of a century less occupied with
empirical than with intellectual discovery. There has been so
much talk of the Elizabethan age, so little of those which
followed, for all that they are more significant, less deceptive
to us in our extremity. Shakespeare was fifty-two when he
died, and the great part of his work was done before even
that forty-ninth year which Aristotle regarded as marking the
peak of human development; it is reasonable to suppose that
if he had not thus been carried off he might have had another
twenty years in which he could, if he wished, have had a
second career in a literary scene which, if it had not the
flaming individual talents of the Elizabethan age, had yet a
rare integrity and obstination in hard thinking. It might well
have been that even if (as on Mr. Eliot's view, for example)
Shakespeare was prevented, by the very candescence of the
poetic process, from setting forth any part of whatever opinion
he may himself have held upon absolute problems or upon
those of everyday, there might have come a whole second
career in which he would have treated, in other than dramatic
form, those problems with which the seventeenth century is
associated in the development of the European mind. It is
not fanciful to miss, even among such names as Locke and
Wren and Cromwell and the founders of the Royal Society,
such a hegemony as Shakespeare would have had by right.
And it is among these, rather than among the amphibious
adventurers of the previous age, that the key to this author
will be found for our generation; and not to the author
only, if we accept the dictum of Delacroix just quoted.

Edward Elgar, himself a native of this area, once wrote a set of Enigma variations, avowedly upon an unknown theme, with the intention that someone, having heard the variations, might one day hit upon that theme (a familiar one), which, played in conjunction with those actually written, would reveal new secrets in the work. This theme has never been found, and yet no one has ever, for this reason, failed to enjoy the variations. Let us in this spirit, and without counting too much upon a final solution, examine our own enigma.

[*Drawn by W. Curtis Green, R.A.*

18A   ABBOT'S SALFORD HALL, WORCESTERSHIRE

[*From a Water-Colour of c. 1850*

18B HOUSE IN THE HIGH STREET, TEWKESBURY

II

SHAKESPEARE AND STRATFORD

THE area outlined above is in effect a unit, allowing of one continuous investigation. Within its clear geographical limits it displays an architecture and an economic structure recognisably its own ; a single temperament, inventive, meddlesome, and sanguine, explains its social history. Any stranger could identify this as Drayton's " heart of England," and from this proceed to calling it the England of Shakespeare. Yet what little it has to do with the person of Shakespeare is confined within Stratford and a few surrounding parishes. For this reason, and to answer those unwilling to see this Shakespeare Country as a social concept, an enclosed area in which people have lived with something of Bridges' " masterful administration of the unforeseen," it would be well to justify the identification of Shakespeare with an area largely unknown to him.

Of course it is easily said that Shakespeare, as much as any Jesuit, knew the enduring hold of childhood experience, and on this ground we might strike out from Stratford as far as Coventry (where he probably saw the Miracle sequence) or Kenilworth (where Elizabeth made a progress during John Shakespeare's term as chief alderman of Stratford). But an exact Shakespeare itinerary would consist less in a single cohering block than in many corpuscular items, often (if all conjecture is to be encouraged) remote from our area. Preston and Titchfield, for example, Venice and Heidelberg, are unsuspectedly rich in rumours, while a survey of places evoked in the plays would need a gazetteer of Europe and the Middle East. Nevertheless this is the Shakespeare Country in a sense different from any of these, or again from that in which les Andelys is the Poussin country. For if its connection with the poet is largely traditional, it is nevertheless the country of "the Shakespeares"; less a family than a caste, the bearers of this name, honoured in 1596 by the Company of Heralds, lived nowhere, in any strength, but in our area. The title of Shakespeare Country may thus, though not in the common sense, be called legitimate.

Little is known about Shakespeare; yet when one considers the buzzing of flies about the carcass of every well-documented author, one must think this little—blessedly little. Even in the case of an author, such as Goethe, in whom there is a seemingly complete interpenetration of life and works, inference from one to the other is still a dangerous trade; and with Shakespeare, of whose voluminous understanding no one can do more than unpick an occasional seam, Dickens has put the matter very well. "It is a great comfort, to my thinking," he says, "that so little is known about the poet. It is a fine mystery, and I tremble every day lest something should come out." And Browning discourages those who, contrariwise, infer from works to life:

> "Here's my work: does work discover
> What was rest from work—my life?"

Knowledge of Shakespeare is mostly knowledge picked up by the way, more in the resolution of everyday problems than in the loot of parish registers. Let us, notwithstanding, enter for a moment the dim temples of Shakespearian research, noting in the ambulatory the separate chapels in which Halliwell-Phillips, Cook, and Baker pursue dissimilarly a single aim.

Verstegan wrote in his *Restitution of Decayed Intelligence*, published in 1605, that "Breakspeare, Shakespeare, and the like are surnames imposed upon the first bearers of them for feats of arms." Thomas Fuller construed the name as Histri-vibrans, and more recently Mrs. Stopes, one of the pygmy dragons of Shakespearian scholarship, cites the Italian parallel of Crollalanza. Sir William Dethick, Garter King of Arms, wrote when granting coat-armour to Shakespeare's father that he had heard his "parents and late antecessors were for their faithful and valiant services advanced and rewarded by the most prudent prince Henry VII. of famous memory."

19 A REGENCY TERRACE IN CHELTENHAM

20 PASTURES AT SNITTERFIELD: Where Richard Shakespeare lived in four reigns

Those not of great family regarded surnames, until Tudor times, as individual property, no more heritable than our Order of Merit. Often they were vocational or otherwise impermanent, but where, as in our instance, they were qualitative and coveted, there is a fairer presumption of lineage between bearers of the name, and to the north of Stratford twenty-five Warwickshire villages have Shakespeares on their register.

The agglomeration in Warwickshire of so many whose name is uncommon outside the county presumes a rough kinship, allowing sometimes of vertical descent for two or more generations, but making it quite impossible to trace for the poet any but a largely conjectural line. The least dangerous inferences are those based on inherited property, and on that assumption we may put forward as an ancestor of William Shakespeare a landowner called Adam de Oldiche, living at Temple Balsall early in the fourteenth century.

Adam de Oldiche was a considerable proprietor, and it is indeed a consistent feature of this theory of the poet's descent that his ancestors were gentry, often well connected but removed from wealth by the accidents of birth in a system of primogeniture. Between Adam de Oldiche and Adam Shakespeare, who in 1389 and till 1414 held land by military service on the estate of Baddesley Clinton, a connection is assumed on the ground of conventional descent by Christian name. Adam Shakespeare, who held the Baddesley Clinton land until 1441, was under age at his father's death, and it is presumed that the land owned in 1457 by Richard Shakespeare, grandfather of the poet, at Temple Balsall, and called 'The Woldiche,' was in fact the portion descended from Adam de Oldiche and bequeathed by Adam Shakespeare to Richard Shakespeare as his son by an earlier marriage. No other line of descent can be attributed to the poet from this stock, for John Shakespeare, supposed brother to the grandfather of the poet, left the neighbourhood and is found at Rowington in 1460, while, of his two sons, one founded the branch of the family found at Wroxall in 1464, while the other, having no male heir, divided the land at Baddesley Clinton between his sons-in-law, Huddespit and Rakley.

Shakespeare is too often spoken of as if he emerged, shining and unprecedented, from a provincial sty. But even such a nibbling inquiry as this has shown the male Shakespeares as a vigorous tribe, always ready, while retaining their inherited lands, to double prosperity by infiltration into un-known areas ; uneven, perhaps (Shakespeares leave bills unpaid, commit nuisances, kill themselves, and are buried at cross-roads with cloven bellies), but nevertheless bold and acquisitive, a people in whom it is hard to discern Sir Sidney Lee's rutting peasantry. Nor were the female Shakespeares kitchen-beasts, living in Greek subjection to their men. They had the entry to religious houses, and in these could rise until they had the administration of wealthy diocesan estates. And for this, as Eileen Power pointed out, they must have been of gentle birth, for just as the monasteries were, like our colonial service, a refuge for younger sons, so an ambitious and cold-blooded girl could reach, in a nunnery, a more than domestic eminence. Thus the Isabella Shake-speare who was prioress of Wroxall Benedictine nunnery in 1500 was a considerable person. When she held court in 1507, landowners as affluent as John Shakespeare came to her and rented a part of her land (in his case " one messuage, four crofts, and a grove "). In 1525, a Jane Shakespeare, who died in 1576, was sub-prioress of this nunnery, and it is therefore plain that Shakespeares owned and administered enough of the wealth and authority of Warwick to make them, not a set of labourers, but a sizeable yeoman force in the county.

Shakespeare was half Arden, and the Ardens had held land in Warwickshire from the time of Edward the Confessor. They were very substantial property-owners and prominent in the official business of the county. Edward Arden, a cousin of the poet, was sheriff of Warwick in 1575, and his house, Park Hall, near Salford Priors, had been for generations the seat of affluent Ardens from whom it is possible to decipher an immediate line to the Snitterfield Ardens into whom the poet's father married. A Robert Arden had been bailiff of Snitterfield in the middle of the fifteenth century, and through four reigns Richard Shakespeare lived at Snitterfield and was tenant of at least 100 acres of Arden land. The village itself had been a big one, and had a fair and market as early as 1242. The poet's great-grandfather, Thomas Arden, lived at Wilmcote, in that parish of Aston Cantlow where Shakespeare is thought to have been married, and from his close relations with several important neighbours it can be assumed that he was, in fact, a younger son of Sir Walter Arden of Park Hall. Such a hypothesis explains why Sir Robert Throckmorton should have been willing to stand feofee to him as well as to Sir Walter, why he inherited little beyond this local good-will, and why Shakespeare himself should bewail the lot of the younger son—in Orlando, for example—and call Falstaff's followers " discarded, unjust serving men, younger sons of younger brothers, and ostlers tradefallen." For there is no doubt that Park Hall was a rather grand house and that, honourable as John Shakespeare's station was, it was decidedly that of a yeoman ; and Shakespeare, though indifferent to luxury, delighted in cultivated talk. His father had made a solid match, but spent his time with the Quineys and Sadlers, whereas his father-in-law lived in a society which, though not better, was more highly evolved, allowing of membership of the Middle Temple and visits to the Holy Land.

The Stratford in which John and Mary Shakespeare lived was a " thoroughfare town," near enough to Watling Street, Fosse Way, and Icknield Street to earn from any Guide Michelin of that date an approving " vaut le détour." With Coventry and Warwick it was one of the three largest towns in the county ; and few towns could show so powerful and ancient a system of self-government by guild. One of its officers said in 1389, " the gild has lasted, and its beginning was, from time whereunto the memory of man reacheth not " ; not the townspeople only, but great merchants from other counties, professional men and nobles, once even a brother of the reigning monarch, were members, and by the late fifteenth century it maintained a formidable oligarchic grip upon the citizen, from the time when he attended its school, through that at which (with its approval) he took up a trade, and for the whole of his professional life. Later, when corporation between traders became vertical (specialised, and between members of a single trade) rather than horizontal and embracing all indifferently, this guild, the double of that in *Die Meistersinger*, lost much of its importance. Something of the Renaissance emphasis on the individual took its place, and Sir Hugh Clopton in particular left on the town a mark far more evident than that of Shakespeare. A bachelor Lord Mayor of London in 1492, he devoted his fortune to his native town, and built, for example, the house called New Place, which Shakespeare later bought, and the great fourteen-

C

arched bridge of freestone, by which a journey to Stratford was robbed of all hazard.

John Shakespeare is first detected at Stratford in 1552, when he is fined for leaving ordure in front of his house. A little before this the Reformation and the marauding official-dom connected with it left the town without responsible government until, in 1553, Edward VI. allowed a petition from the leading burghers for a charter of self-government. The guild, reconstituted as a municipal corporation, offered the liveliest possibilities to an ambitious citizen, for it combined the form, elastic and unburdened with precedent, of a new institution with the wealth and developed resources of an old. Its power extended into every department of the citizen's professional and domestic life. Indeed it is difficult to see how merriment can ever have been considered the essential of Tudor times, for the powers of the guild, if strictly enforced, could have made of the inhabitants a subject people. Its officers were a proprietary body, and deliberated in secret session. The estates and chattels of both guild and college passed into the hands of the new body, and bailiff, vicar, and steward became its auxiliary officers. Personal liberty was not a Tudor concept, and it was impossible to wear what one pleased, abuse one's own family, send one's servant on an errand after dusk, or to have whom one pleased to stay in one's own house. Professional liberty was equally limited. But against all this an energetic and successful man could rise quickly to a position of authority, even if, as in the case of Shakespeare's father, he had come to the town only a few years earlier.

The reconstruction of historical scenes is immensely more difficult than most people suppose, and this particularly in the case of times and places apparently close to our own. For whereas Mediterranean countries in general offer resistance to change, so that it is possible, by visiting towns in Algeria, to experience very nearly the sensations of one entering a suburb of Augustan Rome, the post-Renaissance of northern Europe has evolved at such a pace that it is self-deception to suppose that Shakespeare's surroundings are more accessible than those of the Seneca to whom his contemporaries compared him. Technics apart, it is impossible for those even who have never heard of them, not to be conditioned away from Tudor habits of thought by the work

21 ASTON CANTLOW, WARWICKSHIRE:
Where Shakespeare's parents are said to have been married

22 THE CHANCEL OF STRATFORD CHURCH:
With the poet's monument

23   THE GUILD HALL AND CHAPEL, STRATFORD

of Descartes, Wesley, Rousseau, and the Jacobean Bible. All observations about Shakespeare's life and times are therefore of limited value to any real understanding of him.

In 1530, no Shakespeare was known in Stratford, but in 1552 he was fined for the offence mentioned above. There were few shops, in our sense, and a town indeed was often no more than a protective alliance, grouped round the manor-house, of those small landowners who did not care to live in isolation and without a moat or other defence. Thus many farmers, though living in town, kept beasts there, and otherwise made their homes nearly self-sufficient; and the refuse accumulated by this mode of living, though usually taken in time to their holdings outside the town, added to the filth and confusion of the streets. Thus John Shakespeare would probably have removed his own heaps to his land at Ingon, for there was no incongruity, but rather an example of general practice, in his at once living off the land and engaging in trade. His interest in his inherited lands caused him at one period to be styled " the Agricola of Snitterfield." In 1556, a year in which he is called " a glover " in the law-reports, he brings a claim revealing himself the proprietor of quantities of barley; and his success in these multiple enterprises is proved by the fact that in this same year, after living for some time as a lodger in Henley Street, he bought two freehold tenements, one in Greenhill and the other in Henley Street. He continued, however, to live in his original house in Henley Street, and did not become its owner until he bought it and its neighour in 1575. His rise to power was abrupt, and made easier by marriage to Mary Arden, who had recently inherited from her father. This is presumed to have occurred in 1557, for in the previous year she was unmarried, and in the year following she had a daughter, christened in September; Aston Cantlow (21) is traditionally the scene of this wedding. In 1557 he became ale-taster to the guild, and supervised all traffic in ale and beer and loaves. He was then successively one of the four constables and one of the four affeerors, directing the watch in the former office, and in the latter exercising a rough magistracy over cases in the court-leets for which no express penalties were prescribed. None of these offices was honorary, and the supervision of trade was particularly important in a growing town to which adventurers, finding commerce more lucrative than agriculture, were often attracted ; the officers of the guild at once protected the consumer and maintained a level of professional honour, by which the sale of shoddy cloth and leather, the substitution of horse-hide for ox-hide, and the manipulation of supply of corn in order to exact an inflated price, were heavily punished. The ruin of John Shakespeare is attributed to dearths of which he had to take the full blow. From 1561–64 he was Chamberlain, and presented the accounts of the town in such excellent order that even after his retirement he was sometimes called in to audit the accounts of his successors. It is difficult in this connection to believe the theory of his illiteracy, for not only was this uncommon among his son's generation, but the establishment of complicated accounts and the inspection of those of others could hardly have been done to everyone's satisfaction if he were unable either to write out the one or to read the other. The vocational mark, moreover, which he puts in lieu of signature on many documents, was rather a common convention than a proof of illiteracy. There are in fact many cases (those, for example, of Adrian Quiney, Edmund Hathaway, Henry Wilson, and Richard Boyce) in which mark and signature are used indifferently.

The town was in constant change, and during John Shakespeare's term as Chamberlain, the Guild Chapel (23), for example, was disfigured by Protestants, the " images " being defaced, crosses hacked, the rood-loft taken down, a partition erected between nave and chancel, and a communion board put in place of the altar. In this revised building such early Nonconformists as Cartwright and Throgmorton preached in 1586–87. In the Guildhall again, where John Shakespeare sat as Bailiff and Chief Magistrate, the schoolroom was made out of the old guild " dorter."

In 1565 John Shakespeare became alderman, on the expulsion of William Bott, a Coventry capitalist, and three years later, bailiff. In 1571 his career reached its brief climax when he was elected chief alderman. Municipal office was expensive, and he was no longer a prosperous man. Such variations were common in a developing society, and his namesake, John Shakespeare the corviser, for example, who had been a constable and ale-taster and master of the shoe-maker's company in 1585, had in 1587 to receive a loan from Oken's Charity, and in 1594 left Stratford for Warwick.

Conceivably, Alderman Shakespeare's energies had been diverted from his business, but more probably the balance of his trade, normally weighted equally between gloves, barley, sheep, meat, skins, wool, and leather, was disturbed either by speculation in corn or by a string of indifferent harvests. In any case he ceased to attend council meetings, and though he still made frequent appearances in courts of law, these were now as debtor rather than as creditor; moreover, he was unable to go to church for fear of arrest, and in 1586 was formally relieved of all official status. Nevertheless, the poet also was often in debt, and it is difficult to find evidence of any but legal conduct on John Shakespeare's part during his misfortune—nothing, indeed, more culpable than the fine imposed on him twenty years earlier for failing to keep clean his gutters. He was, moreover, unfortunate in that his wife's estate of Ashbies (a house at Wilmcote and sixty acres of land) accrued to him only after much litigation, and had soon to be mortgaged to Edmund Lambert, a connection of the Ardens, just as his interest in the Snitterfield properties had to be sold to one of his nephews. In 1586 a writ issued for the distraint of his land went for nothing because he had nothing on which he could be distrained.

It is possible to make of these facts some idea of Shakespeare's father, but it is impossible and even impudent to say that we have of Shakespeare himself any reliques which add up to the poet. All that we can do is to pick out those elements in his father's career which necessarily affected Shakespeare as a boy : these are such as the fact of his living in the country so that his children could go angling, follow the hare, distinguish a dozen kinds of apple, and lay out a kitchen-garden—the plateau above Snitterfield was famous for flowers and nightingales ; such as his living in this part of the country, at the junction of Roman roads, in an area thick with castles and the tradition of proud living, a fertile and ambitious plain. His son must have known the impermanent sweets of privilege ; his family had been rich, and was not ; his father had been powerful, and was not ; he must have had friends killed by the plague, burnt by the fires, and drowned by the floods that often overran the town. Of the world outside Stratford he knew less, but not nothing ; the fate, for example, of Edward Arden must have apprized him of the violence of public life. Edward Arden had in-

herited Park Hall in 1563, and in 1575 was high sheriff of
Warwickshire.   He was thus Shakespeare's most important
kinsman and the head of one side of his family.   Like many
Ardens, he persisted in Roman Catholicism, and maintained
in his estate a priest, disguised as a gardener.   He was proud
and outspoken, speaking of Leicester, for example, as an
upstart adulterer, and refused to wear his livery during
Leicester's residence in Kenilworth Castle.   In 1583 his son-in-
law became inflamed by the case of Mary Queen of Scots
and set off for London intending to assassinate Elizabeth.
When seized and set on the rack, he implicated Edward Arden
as the instigator of his plot.   Leicester had Arden prosecuted
with the greatest savagery, and his severed head was later
speared for show on London Bridge.   (This, originally a
disgrace, soon became a coveted mark of rank.)   Shakespeare,
as a player, was much involved in Court intrigue, and he was
thus early aware of its hazards.

John Shakespeare is often said to have been a Roman
Catholic, but the evidence is largely in his failure to attend
the parish church, and this, as has been said, may have a
more temporal significance.   The mutilation of the church
by Protestants during his term as Chamberlain argues also
against this view, and Catholicism is more profitably sought
among the Ardens.   The question has importance in that a
recusant would probably not have sent his son to the guild
school.   Admittedly there were many fine houses about
Stratford at which a lively boy could live very pleasantly in
tutelage, and acquire that dash and cultivation which make
such a miracle of *Love's Labour's Lost*.   But there is no real
ground for supposing Shakespeare did not attend the school,
of which the curriculum is reflected in his familiarity with
Horace and happy choice of Greek names; and, moreover,
intellectual society in London was convulsed, during Shakespeare's rise to celebrity, by just such questions as irrigate
Love's Labour's Lost—the arrival, from 1590 onwards, of many
refugee language teachers, the malicious parody of these by
Shakespeare's countryman and contemporary, John Eliot.
There is, in fact, no need to antedate any stage in the poet's
development.

Most operative of all these facts is the regular appearance
of players in Stratford, for these came at least once a year,
and in 1597, when Shakespeare was thirty-three, there were

24 THE WAY TO HOLY TRINITY CHURCH, STRATFORD

25 THE AVON BY THE CHURCH, STRATFORD

four companies and in addition a puppet show of the city of
Norwich. Players in general lived off the fourteenth- and
fifteenth-century Italian custom by which princes and men of
wealth kept writers and artists and musicians about them, as
much for their own feathering as from concern for the arts.
The ideal of all artists was to be permanently employed in
such a station, and although many, like Jonson, Florio, and
Nashe, secured occasional harbour, those seeking employment for life had often, like Spenser, to have it in exile, or,
like Lyly, to die of the search. Actors were in different case ;
their function was recognised from Christmas until Twelfth
Night, when the various companies would perform at Court
plays selected by the Lord Chamberlain. Each company bore
the name of some nobleman, although he was not responsible
for their subsistence and employed them only occasionally.
Dover Wilson calls this system " a police measure, differing
in kind from personal patronage." Public theatres originated,
in form at least, so that the players might try out their plays
before submission to the Lord Chamberlain, but in fact they
became the chief occupation of the players, and in summer, or
time of epidemic, these would tour the country. In 1586 the
Queen's Players went to the Continent, where they acted for
Frederick II. of Denmark and Christian I., Duke of Saxony.
In 1598 a company of English actors hired the principal
theatre of Paris. There were also local companies. Eight
miles from Stratford, for example, the Earl of Warwick's
players were well known. From 1518–35, again, fourteen
companies visited the monastery of Worcester, including
those of the King and Queen and those of Evesham, Coventry,
Worcester, and Gloucester. Ours was thus an area in which
the practice and appreciation of acting were common. The
lot of the players, though no less precarious then than now,
could be very agreeable, and, as Dover Wilson says, " it has
been too little recognised that the public theatres were in
the main dependent upon the cultured classes of London."
Their audiences were chiefly professional men, students of
the Inns of Courts, and such dashing young peers as South-
ampton and Rutland. (These, moreover, were loyal patrons
of the players ; Rutland as late as 1613 commissioned at Belvoir
an impresa from Shakespeare and Burbage.)

Platter and other itinerists remarked that people in
these times went to the theatre to know what was going

on; so that the career of actor-dramatist was convenient not only for a young man of presence and social ambition, but also for one covetous of power and influence. Actors moved in great houses and yet knew the people's temper; agile as apes, painted as tropical birds, they moved freely about the political jungle. In the great equation of the times, they alone were independent variables. This was an age of success-stories, and Shakespeare must have been familiar with the players whom his father had to entertain. Stratford, as we have seen, was no negligible town, and was, as Leland says, "reasonable well builded of timber," full of travellers, and pleasant enough for a successful man in trade. But Shakespeare was very young, encumbered by an early marriage, unwilling to spend his best years in the support of a declining house. A fire, consuming the wooden houses of Stratford, could put a quarter of its population on poor relief; whereas in London there were palaces of brick and stone, with leaden roofs and pillars of marble and jasper; and as for trade, William Smith, Rougedragon, had said that in London "there is more flesh sold in a day than is sold in Portugal in a whole year." Andrew Boorde, a sixteenth-century itinerist and health-faddist, had said, "there is not Constantinople, Venice, Rome, Florence, Paris, or Cologne cannot be compared to London." Other Stratford men, moreover, had laid successful siege to the capital—Richard Field, for example, the printer to whom Shakespeare entrusted the publication of his poems.

There are many who take any reflection upon Shakespeare's married life almost as a personal affront, and indeed it is difficult to infer in either direction upon the evidence known to us, since this is largely a list of property bought and debts unpaid. But a marriage contracted at eighteen with a woman of no fortune, eight years his senior and several months gone with child, can fairly be called inauspicious. We have in addition an injunction taken out by her kinsman to ensure that Shakespeare could not elude the match. There is, in fact, a fair presumption that Shakespeare's feeling for Stratford was domestic, paternal, and proprietary, but not conjugal. It is in 1596, for example, after the death of his son Hamnet, that he applies to the Herald's Office for a grant of arms to his father. Since his father was barely solvent at this time, this can only mean that Shakespeare was building up for a triumphant return. Possibly, also, his policy of acquiring property at Stratford was an insurance against the conjectural fall of Essex, with whose fortunes he and his company were to some extent identified. In any case, in the following year he bought New Place, the largest house in Stratford, and although he continued to buy property in London until 1613, he was clearly anxious to consolidate his station at Stratford, and to become for its inhabitants, not simply an object of pride and curiosity, but even a kind of ambassador.

Thus in 1598, when the high price of corn at Stratford caused an inventory to be taken, he was found to own eighty bushels of corn and malt. In 1601 his father died, and he began buying freely. In 1602, 107 acres of 4-yard arable land and its adjoining pasture, formerly belonging to the Combes, became his for £320, and from Lady Warwick he bought a cottage in Walker Street and Chapel Lane, which he later gave to his daughter, Susanna. In 1605 he acquired a vested interest in the town's affairs, for he bought for £440 a moiety in the tithes of Stratford, Old Stratford, Welcombe, and Bishopton, on a lease of which thirty-one years had still to run. His share did not in effect exceed a quarter, but it yielded £60 a year, and in addition the tithes in question supported the vicar and paid for the upkeep of the town bridge, the grammar school, and the almshouses, so that Shakespeare, without involving himself in municipal office, became a person of some influence.

Some letters of Abraham Sturley, written in 1598, show how Shakespeare was regarded as the town's leading advocate. These letters come calculatingly from Sturley, who was a great Puritan, a fine Latin scholar, rigidly opposed to tobacco and the theatre ; five years later, indeed, he took advantage of his position as bailiff to suppress all acting in the Guildhall. (Admittedly the plays then on tour were often very different from the " harmless morals " of an earlier generation.) Writing to his brother, Sturley says : " This is one special remembrance from our father's motion. It seemeth by him that our country-man, Mr. Shakespeare, is willing to disburse some money upon some odd yardland or other at Shottery ; he thinketh it a very fit pattern to move him to deal in the matter of our tithes. By the instructions you can give him thereof, and the friends he can make therefore, we think it a fair mark for him to shoot at, and it would do us much good." The town at

D

this time had just suffered from a terrible fire, and this following a dearth of corn. It was thus impossible either to pay the national taxes or to maintain the normal civic services. Shakespeare himself, for example, had sold to the corporation a load of stone for the repair of the Clopton bridge. To Richard Quyney, then staying in London, Sturley wrote suggesting that Shakespeare should speak for the town, and secure for it either a temporary relief from taxation, or a substantial loan.

Five years after this correspondence, Shakespeare's position was considerably improved by his incorporation in the company of nine King's Players. He ranked as a groom of the chamber to James I., and could be required to usher at Court. He wore livery, received a regular salary, and at the Coronation was given nine feet of scarlet cloth and damask for his robes. He moved about constantly in London, often leaving taxes unpaid, and never, whether at Bishopsgate, Bankside, Cripplegate, Southwark, or Blackfriars, living far from the river by which his plays were performed; for this was a waterfront city, like Budapest, and each of the royal palaces stood on its banks, so that, whether to Greenwich, to Richmond, to Whitehall, or to Hampton Court, the monarch could always progress by water, and but, indeed, for the rejection of the Jones-Webb plans for Whitehall Palace, might still do so.

It was in 1610 that the most interesting of his dealings with the corporation occurred. Unfortunately the account available to us of the proposed Combe enclosures is fussy and inconclusive. The family of Combe had grown rich by usury, had become lawyers and had sat in Parliament, had translated " one hundred moral emblems " from the French. John Combe, dying in 1613, left five pounds to Shakespeare. But his nephews, William and John, having an immense capital based on heavy rates of interest, decided to augment this by landlord monopoly and oppression. William Combe attempted, by bullying and oppression, to provoke his tenants into rioting, after which he could lawfully enclose or confiscate their land. John Combe had a record of personal violence.

Any developed agricultural scheme within a small area demands that land be enclosed and put to those specialised uses to which Warwickshire, more than any other county, lends itself. The issue was thus less between enclosure and the persistence of champaign tenure than between humane enclosure and the appropriation of the only means of livelihood open to the people—the depopulation, in short, of whole parishes. Even in 1275 the hedges round the Abbey of Bordesley, in Worcestershire, were regularly torn down, and by the fifteenth century many quite large areas were deserted and their inhabitants living as beggars, highwaymen, or primitive industrialists. Thus in 1381, Arrow and Alcester were infested by brigands, " some of them gentlemen," and in 1401 a commission was set up to arrest those who, masked and with the apparatus of torturers, made travelling an affair of hazard. In the sixteenth century Rous, the antiquary and chantry priest of Warwick, petitioned Parliament, detailing innumerable thefts, till in 1517 Wolsey established a commission to investigate there. In 1586 one man in every twenty-six in Warwick was a beggar, and the precocity of industrial development in this area was partly due to the ready supply of labour on which emigré foreign employers and artificers could draw.

Enclosure at the beginning of the seventeenth century meant either the removal of the one asset by which the people lived, or, less directly, the cessation of essential public services, for the upkeep of these was often provided for by tithes from the common lands. This was particularly irksome in that the people profited not at all from the redistribution, at the Dissolution, of as much as a sixth of the country, and when the lands confiscated from the gunpowder plotters were similarly given as enclosed parks to men already substantially situated, thousands of people rose, in 1607, to protest.

Thus the Combes were not only personally odious, but attempting action contrary to the public interest, when they announced in 1610 the enclosure of the common fields surrounding their Welcombe estate. Such an enclosure would mean that the parish school would be locked against its children, the old people of the parish be turned out of their almshouses, and the great Clopton bridge, source of prosperity and highway to London, fall into disrepair. Public opinion was inflamed, and Shakespeare himself stood directly to lose by enclosure, for he was part tenant of the threatened land. Thus Thomas Greene, town clerk, must have felt confident of success when he approached

D*

Shakespeare in London to invite his intervention, only to find that Shakespeare, having the previous month concluded an agreement with the Combes' agent by which his own interest was guaranteed from harm, refused to turn militant. A formal letter, despatched by the council at Christmas in the same year, had equally little effect, and although an entry in Greene's diary for September of the following year had been construed as marking a change of heart, the argument for inertia is strong. Unless we are to see Shakespeare's attitude as collusive in an unsavoury design, two explanations remain : first, he had the measure of the Combes and knew that (as in fact happened) no court of law would uphold their case, whereas his intervention would involve inconvenient journeys, and would then probably not be decisive ; second, he might well have refused to serve a corporation which had forbidden the exercise of his profession within its walls, and had relieved his father of a well-earned and valuable status.

Shakespeare died, very possibly of an early summer infection, within two years of this. His death caused no stir outside his home-town, and no report of it can be traced to London. A certain proprietary inquisitiveness lingered in the town, and there have been some who, dissatisfied perhaps with Johnson's monument, were for exhuming the body. The local earth was thought to resist the process of decay (King John's body was later exhumed in Worcester Cathedral and found in recognisable condition, while bodies laid in the Quineley vault at Cropthorne do not decay, but wither). The precedent of Burns, again, was quoted, but in the event the body, with its conspicuous towering forehead, was left untouched. The material relics of the poet were not always respected, and in 1759 the Rev. Francis Gastrell, owner of New Place, pulled down the house in which Shakespeare died, having destroyed also the mulberry tree planted by the poet. It is rather to the players that we should give credit for the fitting enthronement of their great colleague, for, from Betterton to Komisarjevsky, it is the practical men of the theatre who have done most for Shakespeare in his native town. As early as 1748, the money required for repairs to William Shakespeare's tomb was raised by a benefit perform-ance of *Othello*, given by a touring company of players.

Betterton indeed was one of the first to make a constructive

26, 27 FARMFIELDS AND VICTORIAN ACHIEVEMENTS
AT TEMPLE GRAFTON

28, 29 SHAKESPEARE MEMORIAL THEATRES: new and old

pilgrimage to Stratford. Previously, itinerists had failed to seize upon the poet. Jean de Blaeu, for example, in his *Théatre du Monde* (1645) mentions only John de Stratford and Sir Hugh Clopton as notable inhabitants of Stratford. But when, in 1709, Nicholas Rowe wanted a biographical preface to his new edition of the plays, he consulted Betterton who, for all that he performed Shakespeare's plays in the versions of Dryden, Shadwell, and Tate, had been at pains to visit Stratford and pick up all that he could about the poet. Betterton was the son of an under-cook of Charles I., and he rose to be, in Cibber's words, " an actor as Shakespeare was an author, without any companion." Pepys thought him " the best actor in the world," and Pope applied to him a phrase of Cicero, " vitae bene actae incundissima est recordatio." Betterton was a leader of advanced Restoration opinion and had been to visit Molière in Paris. Charles II. had lent him, for his part in *Love and Honour*, the robes worn at his Coronation, and he had a long association with Congreve, which proved his salvation when, having lost £8000 in an East Indian speculation, he recouped on the first productions of *Love for Love*, *The Mourning Bride*, and *The Way of the World*.

Similarly in the eighteenth century, Garrick secured much popular recognition both for Shakespeare and for Stratford, as Shakespeare's town. He had many opponents. Some, like Hume, said that Shakespeare showed " a total ignorance of theatrical art and conduct." Others, like the sculptor Nollekens, preferred such spectacles as that of Mr. Rich, who captivated thousands by his " wonderful and singular power of scratching his ear with his foot like a dog." In 1753, Garrick commissioned from Roubiliac a bust of Shakespeare, which he at first housed in a temple built for the purpose in his garden at Hampton, and later presented to the town of Stratford. This, at the time, unusual gesture aroused much enthusiasm both in England and in France, where Patu spoke of " this noble enterprise," and Morellet called Garrick " mon cher Shakespeare " (on another occasion, however, when Morellet ventured a criticism of the actor, Garrick rushed at him and seized him by the throat, calling him repeatedly, " French dog ! French dog ! "). The bust shows Shakespeare's person as if penetrated by that of Garrick, for not only is the pose a favourite one of the actor, but the costume also is contemporary with its execution.

Garrick, like Neville Chamberlain, never travelled without a copy of Shakespeare, and in 1769 he conceived the idea of a great jubilee celebration at Stratford, by which the town would be finally established as a *lieu de pèlerinage*. This project is described in the memoirs of Cradock, an elderly civil servant, gardener, and naturalist, friend of Buffon and Johnson, who at this time was much in green-room society. He was intimate with the Garricks, and two weeks before the chosen day went down to Stratford to inspect the preparations, supposed then to be almost complete. Not merely, however, had the materials for the amphitheatre failed to arrive—they had not yet been bargained for in Birmingham. A large order of lamps, by which the building was to be illuminated, had been destroyed and their glass trodden into the soil. Above all, the townspeople were bitterly suspicious of the whole affair, lived in expectation of looting and burning at the hands of a mob, and refused to collaborate with the sponsors. Garrick was stubborn, and modified his plans only by reducing the entertainment to a mobile pageant and his own recitation of an occasional ode.

On the day preceding the jubilee, the town was packed, and the pilgrims were awakened before dawn by a " serenade of guitars and choruses." After breakfast, Dr. Arne's *Judith* was performed in the church ; the excellent soloists were poorly supported both by choir and audience. There was much ribaldry, and Earl Beauchamp, who arrived during the morning, left before luncheon. A violent storm forced the promoters to abandon the street procession, the costumes for which, being made from miserable stuffs, ran or fell in pieces, despite the efforts of Mrs. Garrick. Meanwhile a local barber, hired to shave and trim the great actor, cut deeply, whether from agitation or malice, into his cheek, so that, as Cradock reports, " while I was bustling with the performers, the ladies applied constant stiptics to stop the bleeding."

The recital of the Ode was a great personal success for Garrick, who, as he stood upon the tongue of land which is now the Bancroft Gardens, was acclaimed by many fashionable admirers. Even during this amiable scene, however, disturbances broke out in the town, so that "the Meynells and other quality," who had come from London, immediately set off on the return journey, trusting in relays of pack-horses to carry them to a place of greater amenity. In the evening a ball and masquerade, designed as the climax to a day of cultivated revelry, was initiated with fair zest by those still at hand ; but this in turn was interrupted by the Avon, which rose abruptly and soon inundated the entire arena. Many of the dancers, whether from the rapidity of the rise or from concentration on the matters in hand, were unaware of their peril until the water was above the floor of their carriages.

Garrick wanted to make Stratford a centre of Shakespearian study, and to establish there a school of acting and elocution ; but this idea occurred to humbler players also. In 1820 a comedian called Charles Mathews presented at Stratford Town Hall a farce, *Country Cousins and the Sights of London*, at the end of which he presented plans for the building by public subscription of a memorial theatre in Stratford. Nothing came of this, and when Benjamin Haydon visited Stratford eight years later, the sites of Shakespeare's birth and burial remained his only monuments. These were, however, enough to overwhelm the painter. " Hail and farewell ! " he wrote. " Not the Loggia of Raphael, or the Chapel of Michaelangelo, will ever give me such native, unadulterated rapture as thy silver stream, embosomed church, and enchanting meadows, O immortal Stratford ! " He maintains throughout this tone of strenuous idealism ; the face of the church-warden, for example, " looked as if not one vicious thought had ever crossed his mind." Fleshly needs became odious to him, and from some of them he felt an immunity which, in these days of rationing, many pilgrims would be happy to share. " I stood and drank in to enthusiasm all that a human being could feel. . . . I was lost, quite lost. As soon as I recovered from my trance I was sorry to walk back to the town to talk to waiters and chambermaids of tea and bread and butter. To feel that they were requisite, to think of eating and drinking at all, was a bore and a disgust."

At the turn of the century, municipal life in Stratford was agitated by quarrels and controversies, which must be examined, because they show perfectly the enduring horror of small-town municipal life. Miss Corelli, around whose dumpy person this brawling occurred, had been advised in 1899 to leave London and live in the country. Her choice of Stratford as a second home, though ambitious, had nothing initially deplorable in it, and much of the look of the town was saved by the liberal distribution of her profits. At first her experiments were modest ; she gave a cup, for example, to the Stratford Boat Club, and many photographs exist of her, surrounded by young men in the narrow white trousers and boots of the period. Tea has been drunk, and a huzza launched upon the evening air. This was very well ; but boating, although it occupied much of her thoughts and caused her to import from Italy, not a gondola merely, with full tackle and trim, but a gondolier as well—boating was not enough. She interfered in the management of the church, and since this was then £900 in debt, she was able, by paying this off, to secure the relegation of a new tablet from the church to the museum. Encouraged by this, and having herself been recently translated by Maurice Rostand into French, she asserted herself as critic, and in 1900 laid about the festival programmes. But it was in 1902 that a proposal was made for a Carnegie library, to be built in Henley Street and to supplement, as a mark of American homage, the Gothic drinking-fountain dedicated by Irving in 1887. This library would occupy the sites of several cottages then adjoining the Birthplace, and its utility and political significance had to be balanced against the loss of these relics. Many people, like Ellen Terry and Alice Meynell, put forward a reasoned case for its rejection ; but Miss Corelli was intemperate. Those who proposed acceptance of the offer were Body-snatchers, organised in a Pro-Beer Party, planning a campaign of looting and alcoholism. If no paper would publish these facts, she must issue her own ; and the *Avon Star*, quickly balanced by the *Errors of the Avon Star*, recalled the methods, though not the brilliance and integrity, of Wilkes' *North Briton.* Many disagreeable facts came out. Mr. Carnegie can hardly have expected, when making his offer, that one of its consequences would be the news that Miss Corelli had not been born in wedlock. One comment only, indeed, is recorded of him throughout this dreary affair : " If Henley Street were as old as Christ," he said, " I'd pull it down."

In the end the library was built, and Miss Corelli, un-daunted by the farthing damages awarded to her in an action for libel, continued to live at Mason Croft alone with Miss Vyver, visited by Mark Twain and the Laboucheres, embraced by Miss Wilcox, conspicuous at the Shakespeare Ball in a costume of brown velvet to which the name " Pansy " was generally accorded. Honour was done to America by her

30 OMBERSLEY FROM ITS CHURCHYARD

31 A PRIMITIVE COTTAGE GROUP

32 THE SEVERN-AVON PLAIN FROM ABOVE GREAT MALVERN

endowment of Harvard House, and to the opening of this
Mary Anderson came. More private excitements filled her
later years ; not, indeed, since the illusory pregnancy of Mary
Tudor had the accessories of passion been so carefully simu-
lated as in the fake romances of Marie Corelli. If it was not
Mr. Arthur Severn, then it was Sir Thomas Lipton ; the one
so urbane, the other owning a yacht driven by steam and

33 CHAMPAIGN FIELD CULTIVATION AT CRIMSCOTE,
NEAR STRATFORD, from the air

weighing several thousand tons ; if this gondola rocked, it
was not from the motion of the Avon.

All this is more nasty than nice. It is of more use to look
for a continuity of ideas, in this area, than to make an addition
of relics. What we see and what Shakespeare saw differ
radically ; his roads, for example, were no better than Albanian
highland tracks ; the towns and villages he saw were not
built only of the black-and-white we recognise to-day, but
also of the remaining buildings of former times ; they were
not regular, and in place of the stepped-back streets we know,

there were casual groups of houses, much as the villages
under Bredon still have ruminant cottages that push their
rumps across the public way. Even such a town as Tewkesbury had not its houses facing the street until the sixteenth
century; previously their entrances were reached by an alley
or a court or even a small tunnel, and many of these still
remain at Tewkesbury and give the town its crenellated air.
But most curious of all to our eye would be the open land,
cultivated by strips and without hedges or any division except
a shallow ditch or a line of turf. This manner of working
the soil survived by several centuries the social system which
first encouraged it; in 1798 there were still 57,000 acres in
Warwickshire alone under open tenure; and a remnant of this
persisted at Whitnash until 1850. Even to-day, at Crimscote,
a few miles from Stratford, there are fields still bearing the
configuration of champaign tenure, and these have been
photographed from the air (33).

Little, in fact, remains from Shakespeare's scene, little
but the great ceremonial elm of Warwickshire, a dozen
kinds of apple and a way of building—half-timber and half-
brick or plaster—the brilliant Irish green of the Avon
valley and the road from Kenilworth to Coventry, and on
the steep sides of Bredon a little untimely flower called Peace
Everlasting. Yet it is difficult to take the ridge road above
Compton Wynyates and not to see with the eyes of John
Speed, the early seventeenth-century itinerist, who said of
this prospect, "from Edgehill we may behold another Eden,
as Lot did the plain of Jordan before that Sodom fell." We
who have seen the fall of many cities and heard the barbarian
at our gates have still this other Eden, than which no other
landscape more surely reflects the enduring temper of our
race.

III

SOCIAL AND ECONOMIC HISTORY

SCENERY is too often described in æsthetic terms, as if it were not lived in and worked on and fought over but just looked at for two months in the year by people on holiday. Such descriptions neither bring the scene before those who have never seen it, nor satisfy those in whose memories it has once been immobilised. I notice, moreover, that although after reading Homer, for example, or Tolstoy, one has the clearest idea of the landscape in which one has read of action, yet of this landscape only the barest account appears in the text—a few epigraphs between major events, or three recurrent double-adjectives. From this I have been led to see more use in putting the mechanics of our landscape before the reader than in attempting what in effect is a distinct and arduous genre.

Our area contains no raw country, nothing that has not been gone over again and again by man and is not best spoken of in terms of his achievement. Its social history is one of generous initial provision, kept up and augmented by people who have never hesitated to admit those people or things from outside whose fortune might supplement their own. It is a lesson in social development to see how this people, so far from in-breeding to preserve the abundance of its gifts, has always welcomed the adhesion of foreign ideas. No area is more English than this in which the almshouses of Warwick were endowed by Nicholas Eifler, a Westphalian, the wool-weaving trade learnt by the Saxons from Flemish artisans, the armoury trade built up from Dutch models under William III., the Stourbridge glass industry set up by Hungarians in the sixteenth century, the cart-horses bred from

35

Zeeland stock introduced by Lord Chesterfield, and the immense market-gardens of Evesham originated by a Genoese ambassador. To this centre of England (Coventry is equidistant from London, Hull, Bristol, and Liverpool) there came Danes, from Watling Street; earlier the Cornavii had invested it; here, in the seventh century, the English and the Saxon invaders coalesced; the Oddinsell family, a powerful fourteenth-century industrial unit, were Flemish. Many Jews lived in Warwick, Coventry, and Worcester, and after the Edict of Nantes, Huguenots became the leading craftsmen of Coventry. Nor was this involuntary. In the twelfth

[Drawn by W. H. Bartlett

34 BABLAKE HOSPITAL, COVENTRY, 1830

century, Coventry enticed new merchants with her charter of liberties, and after the Restoration, Birmingham, almost alone among important centres, was not a corporate town, and could offer to dissenting craftsmen asylum from the Act of Uniformity. These are procedures different alike from the unwitting occasional reception of foreign talent, and from that organised contact with Europe by which, from time to time in the Middle Ages, after the Field of the Cloth of Gold, under Henry VIII., or after James I. had brought about a truce between Holland and Spain, all areas were enriched. Through these, for example, there came to Gloucester in the early twelfth century a candlestick (now in the Victoria and

Albert Museum) so similar both to those made under Bernwald at Hildesheim, and to that on view since the thirteenth century at Milan, that it is an epitome of this interpenetration. Similarly, when agriculture was impoverished from the loss at the Reformation of the ingenious care with which the monks, predominant in our area as nowhere else, had kept up their vast estates, new life was brought by contact with Dutch models.

Such an attitude lives off a consciousness of favour, of being able to dispose of uncommon resources. No one can travel in this area without being aware of the advantage taken of its extreme and constructive variety. Around Evesham, for example, where the soil is particularly good, there is such a luxuriance of fruit that one is reminded of the feather-bright plain of olive-trees below Troy, and at blossom-time a walker in this head-high forest can go for miles and know full daylight only as a remote brilliance, six avenues off. This was always so : forty Roman camps have been traced within six miles of Evesham, and each one enclosed and palisaded, not in war but for husbandry. The evidence of coins has shown that armies led there by Claudius in A.D. 43 remained in continuous occupation till the departure of the Romans in 410. From this black soil corn was exported between 280–350 to the Rhine valley, just as it was sent in 1549 to starving Bristol, and bought in 1574 by Thomas Sackford, victualler for Ireland. Across in Warwickshire the harvests of the Middle Ages were so full that much fresh labour had to be got in. But the glory of this neighbourhood is its fruit ; that cider, which St. Augustine preferred to all other drinks, has always been made in the area which he is thought to have visited, and Worcestershire cider has always been equal even to the legendary brands of other areas—that, for example, made at Évreux around 1660. A plumb dropped anywhere in history will drag up some reference to this most fortunate part. One reads of the London soldiers' delight in the abundance of fruit on which they happened while campaigning in 1644 ; in the twelfth century, William of Malmesbury praises Worcestershire vineyards ; or there is, in the eighteenth century, a whole literature of Pomona, and in the boastful sixteenth such a catalogue of riches as would be hard to excel even now—and these not by genera only, but with many named species. There were seventy kinds of apple : Under-

E

leaf, Foxwhelp, Magdalen, and Go No Further ; Red Muscle and Mirabilon and forty-two other kinds of plum, and a hundred sorts of vine, of which the Frontiniac, Blood Red, and D'Arbois were most admired. This considered, it comes as no surprise that the device of the Worcestershire men at Agincourt was " a pear-tree laden with fruit."

An area in which the Paradise Apple grows wild is one in which a living is evidently won with some co-operation from Nature, and therefore particularly attractive to small property owners. By Domesday it had been entirely manorialised, and in 1796 William Marshall reports it as recognisably the beau ideal of the gentleman farmer. " The district abounds," he says, " in the higher yeomanry, gentlemen cultivating their own estates of £200–£500 a year." Yet this area, seemingly designed for the *ferme ornée*, became so only after centuries of hard, and often of unenlightened, labour ; Marshall admits that in his time no farmers in the country were more eager for technical improvement than these. The area is in fact developed, as much as endowed, and its wealth goes far beyond (and, in the quarries and mines of the north, beneath) the quality of the soil. Yet this, which may everywhere (except in the Bunter sandstone area of N.W. Worcestershire) be turned with abundant profit, is its most consistent asset. Even in the densely wooded Arden of Warwickshire, for example, land exposed during the early eighteenth century levelling of trees for the iron furnaces, proved as fertile as that of the southerly Feldon.

It is difficult to treat satisfactorily of the economic history of our area except in relation to water-courses. For most areas have obvious features by which they can be made known to a mapless reader. If political boundaries, frontiers or neutral zones or evident changes of language, currency, and habits do not suffice, then there are natural limits to a single enquiry. A line of mountains or a major river puts an end to the surveyor's task as surely as a day's walking formerly marked the end of a parish. None of this, however, applies to our case. For a barrier of speech, we should have to go well outside to the west ; and although the Malverns (32, 130), the oval hump of Bredon (7, 137), and the long, stony arm of the Cotswolds are conspicuous everywhere, it is rather to the great rivers of the area that its prosperity may be most fittingly accounted. On these, indeed, it depended

35 BLOSSOM-TIME NEAR EVESHAM

36 AT KINSHAM, NEAR TEWKESBURY

37   UPTON

38   WORCESTER

SEVERN TOWNS

for transport at times when roads, controlled by no central authority, fell into nobody's keeping, and Elizabeth herself, *en route* for Shrewsbury, could get no farther than Coventry. County boundaries, for our purpose, would be least satisfactory of all; for these, nowhere ideal, are in our case particularly absurd, in that floating islets of one county have to be fished out of another, and a diagram of the whole resembles less a self-sufficing rural area than a preliminary experiment of Mendel. Nash, indeed, thought this problem soluble only by the adoption of the gazetteer form, and Habington was much hampered in his researches by the fact that, being on oath not to leave the county, he was unable to visit many of these outlying particles, and had to peer at them across stretches of alien soil.

The Severn is an adult river, between whose tall banks a great volume of mountain water flows at a speed favourable enough to export traffic and the working of mills, but fatal to unwary travellers. Both Severn and Avon have murderous histories, and not stray travellers only and their carriages, but whole villages and a multitude of trees have disappeared beneath their flood; the Clopton bridge at Stratford, and that built after Agincourt at Marton by John Middleton, not only gave these towns a window upon the great world and saved them from tolls, but also preserved many lives. Even to-day the Severn is treacherous as Tiber, and all lovers of the cinema will have seen the Biblical gala of the Severn Bore, in which a great ruff of water rushes up-river at a height and speed which, though considerable enough, never quite equal one's expectation. The Bore, called by some " the water war," reaches its peak near Elmore and a few miles below Gloucester, and had formerly a most respectful audience. It is not, in fact, sixty years since a spectator was reminded by it of " the wall of water forced back when the Israelites made their miraculous passage of the Red Sea." It was " an emblem of velocity," he thought, and revealed to him the meaning of the phrase, " the voice of many waters." Many of the most exciting things about the Severn do not strictly concern us—the trapping of eels in wicker putchins, for example, the little harbours of Sharpness and Lydney, and the shallow painted cliffs at Aust and Fretherne. Our aspects are homely, but lucrative; there is the excellent mustard on which Falstaff remarks, which is found on the Mythe Tute

at Tewkesbury, and the coarse fishing above this point.
The woad of Tewkesbury was a licensed industry even in
1594 ; but more important for us is the confluence of mountain
streams which, joining the original stream soon after it leaves
Plinlimmon, soon reach a depth and velocity easily put to
profit by a developing mountain area. Thus it was that the
area was independent of Roman roads from medieval times,
and that canals rather than roads were built by Brindley in
the eighteenth century to link it with the ports and collieries
of England. Thus it was that Coventry, being on none of
these routes, complained of a land-lock.

The river has hardly entered Worcestershire at Upper
Arley before it rushes powerfully through Bewdley. No town
more amply than Bewdley justifies the apostrophe of Habington to the Severn, for its former wealth and present beauty
proceed entirely from the river ; its many eighteenth-century
shops and warehouses, its elegant bridge by Telford, its
church " in the Italian style," and the excellently severe bow-
fronted houses (that, for example, of Prattinton the antiquary)
all pay tribute to the " greatest water ornament and prodigal
benefactor of our country." (Not rivers only, but canals,
brought a similar prosperity : for the completion of Brindley's
Staffordshire canal, offered to Bewdley and refused by the
townspeople, was no sooner established at Stourport in 1771—
then marked by a solitary inn in a barren and sandy area—than
a sizeable town instantly arose.)

Much traffic flowed through Bewdley as early as the
fourteenth century, and its tolls, against which Gloucester
and Bristol petitioned in 1412, brought in a handsome revenue.
It is at this point that the river assumes its deep and final
course, and Bewdley was thus not only a capital for a manufacturer to set up his workshop, but also a centre for embarka-
tion, and the town buzzed with activity. As many as 400
pack-horses put up there overnight. Caps and combs were
made, and leather, timber, corn, flannel, and wool sent rolling
down-stream to Bristol. It was also an administrative centre,
and the Council of the Welsh Marches sat more than once at
Tickenhill. If enclosures pressed less hardly here than elsewhere, it was because those unemployed as a result of them
could always be absorbed into the woollen industry (8000
people were maintained by it in the middle of the fifteenth
century) ; and when this industry declined, there was imposed

upon it, in 1570, what amounted to government maintenance, for woollen caps were made compulsory on Sundays and holidays, and from this Bewdley profited before all other towns.

The Severn was not only a carrier of wealth but itself a source of it, for no river in the kingdom was more full of fish. Nash remarks how, by the eighteenth century, these had been largely exhausted by intensive fishing, and the river came to contain chiefly sea-going fish—salmon, shad, and lamprey. Salmon indeed was so plentiful that the parents of the apprentices used often to stipulate in their agreements that the boys were not to receive salmon more than twice each week. As late as 1826 it was one of the *plats régionaux* of Cheltenham ("a white, muddy substance between the more solid red parts marks the high perfection of the Severn salmon"). Previously there had been lamperns, held by some the equals of those caught at the mouth of the Seine, near Harfleur, and favoured by Henry V., while the lamperns of Worcestershire were stewed and sent in the eighteenth century to the Empress of Russia. This fish, though often used simply as a bait for cod, was a delicacy, and classed by Linnæus among *amphibia nantia*, for their system of breathing (through seven holes in the side of their necks) is adapted to both land and water.

The Avon betrays even by its name (one common to many gently-flowing streams) that, against the Severn, it is an amateur among rivers, burdened with no rare fish, supporting no infant industries, unable even to maintain a straight course, recalling in its perversity the paraphrase of W. J. Turner :

> " Shall I compare thee to a summer's day ?
> Thou art more lovely and more indolent."

Even the Stour is more in place in a chapter of economic history, for its shallow, scarcely moving waters were long held the source of that particular fastness which distinguished, between 1720–60, the silks and carpets and pretty flowered stuffs of Kidderminster. The Salwarpe also could carry barges, and from 1378 the town of Droitwich took out a licence for levying tolls upon this traffic. In these circumstances the Avon could not be allowed to remain ineffectual, and in the fourteenth century, Richard Beauchamp, Earl of Warwick, wished it to be made navigable as high as Warwick, in order that wine for himself might come up, and merchandize,

to the profit of his county, go down. This was already true
of the Severn, and by 1577 the city of Worcester thought
it a common trust to scour and deepen its channel, so that
the coal-boats, of which the first arrived in 1570, might come
in greater numbers. Road traffic depended on the continence
of these rivers, which, by overflowing the fords on which
all major roads converged, could delay traffic for weeks.

This improvement of water transport set problems, not
only of engineering, but of social development. All schemes
necessarily cut across private property, arousing in opposition many whose interests, trifling in proportion to the whole,
might easily be paramount in a minor issue. Just as the
history of mining and quarrying in this area presents cases of
oppression and treachery as savage as anything in Engels, so
the history of its waterways is as full of sabotage and mis-
calculation as that of Panama. In a feudal society, or one
based on monopolistic capitalism, anything can be forced
through ; but as it was, now an enlightened druggist, now a
retired officer, now an aspiring landowner, set out on plans
which, from incompetence, lack of funds, or the malicious
intervention of subsidiary powers, came to nothing. In
1635, William Sandys of Fladbury envisaged a scheme by
which the Avon should be navigable even during those summer
months when boats could not get up on the Severn as far as
Worcester. This meant forty miles of digging and clearing ;
many acres of land, and the businesses established on them,
had to be bought at forced prices. Thirteen locks were built,
to adjust the declension of the stream, and work round existing
mills. Boats of thirty tons' burden could then move freely under
sail, and on calm days were drawn by ropes whose friction is
still perceptible on the bridges of Pershore and Eckington.

The Civil War discouraged further experiment, and even
in 1655 the position was so unsettled that Andrew Yarranton,
one of the best of contemporary engineers, and a man whose
work altered the look of this area only less than did that of
Brindley, refused an offer of part-ownership in the projected
canal from Droitwich to the Severn, holding out for £750
cash. This extension of the Salwarpe was not, like most
such projects, an attempt to stimulate new or flagging industries,
for the production of salt was among the oldest and most
stable of trades, and its distribution alone was thought to
require attention. At the Restoration many plans were

39 DIDBROOK, GLOUCESTERSHIRE

40 KINVER EDGE FROM WYRE FOREST

41 FORD'S HOSPITAL, COVENTRY

[*From an Aquatint after a Drawing by W. Mason*

42 COVENTRY RACECOURSE IN THE LATE
EIGHTEENTH CENTURY

considered, and in 1665, Lord Windsor undertook to push through to the Severn by a string of six locks—a plan found to be impracticable only when five out of six were completed. In the same year, Yarranton's canal from Stourbridge to Kidderminster was opened. This, like many others, had no official support, and was finished only by the temerity of its designers and their confidence in ultimate success; the locking of Dick Brook was also Yarranton's work.

By the eighteenth century roads had improved enough to make their maintenance a matter of public pride. Yet in 1773 the road between Droitwich and the Severn was still unusable for nine of the year's twelve months. Not Severn and Avon only, but the Teme as well, could now carry certain necessary loads, and the salt traders, having no regular outlet for their product, were open to schemes of fantasy, such as the immense brine-pipe which some were anxious to build from Droitwich to Hawford. A Bill for it was put up in 1708, and £12,000 expended on it by an apothecary named Baker; but, having no legal authority, he could not complete his venture.

The canal era, coming at the end of the eighteenth century, gave to the areas affected the utility of a great river exactly adjusted to existing needs. The Severn could now transport farm produce — hay and hops and clover-seed — and this although no advance had been made in traction, which was still by gangs of men. The canal brought, not only these new and old amenities, but also a curious social cachet; for it was thought very dashing to give water-parties, and at Stourport in 1775 these " regattas " (itself a new word) were constantly rolling past a goggling populace. One of them, starting from Tickenhill and stuffed with the pick of the county, had on board a concert of French horns, and was met, as it passed under the new bridge, with a salute of guns.

Eight Acts were passed between 1766–91, for the building of canals in the county, each the cause of lively disputes. Many meetings were held, but the opposition of landowners, though in one case backed by as much as £20,000, could only delay the execution of schemes so clearly to the advantage of all. If there was nothing to mark the completion of any of these canals on the same scale as the commissioning from Verdi of *Aïda* for the inauguration of Suez, there was all the same a general outburst of bell-ringing, bonfire-burning, and promiscuous junketing. Nor were the results less satisfactory. The Droitwich canal returned each year 15 per cent. of its entire cost; not to Stourport alone, but to Pershore, Tewkesbury, Upton, Evesham, and many other towns came profits of which visible tokens remain in the fine brick-built houses and converted wharfs of the period. Canals did not merely join one great town with another, as Birmingham with Worcester, but towns with the sources of their raw material—mines, quarries, and timber-yards. Huge crowds came to see such novelties as the iron barges of Stourport, and river traffic, by which one horse could do the work of fifty by road, became so general that in 1814 the towing-path below Worcester was open to draught horses. Thus, although not all schemes came through (that from Leominster to Stourport could not tunnel through the crumbling soil near Mamble), immense invention and energy were applied; steam vessels appeared at Worcester, and for the Worcester–Birmingham canal a special perpendicular lift was devised, though not in the event used, to reduce the chain of fifty-six locks required for this prince among canals. Many companies were founded, and the stability of these made clear the foresight of the young Duke of Bridgewater who, in the days after the South Sea Bubble, had fixed on the canal as the safest market for small investors.

Roads improved as sharply as waterways, and the problems of coaching, like those of barge-hauling, were in large measure solved just at the time when they were made obsolete by the invention of railways. Telford and Macadam had so improved the foundation and metalling of roads that the journey from Birmingham to London, which in 1731 took two and a half days, was done in seven and a half hours. The coaches put up a spirited fight to retain the carriage of mails, and in 1838 their drivers had to be threatened with the treadmill as punishment for furious driving. On the loss of this coveted traffic in 1839, coaching instantly declined; within two years the toll-gate at Bromsgrove lost half its revenue, and many inns were forced to close.

The railway systems introduced a new orientation, by which the riverside towns were robbed of their advantage, and in some cases of their whole purpose, whereas the industrial blocs were in effect finally established, for railways are expensive and their services indispensable, and few firms can afford to set up away from their lines. Therefore, though many of the most interesting parts of our area are inaccessible by rail, this is not wholly a misfortune, since the effect of new services might be to destroy that which they would take us to see. Stratford is on no main line, and Deerhurst, Baginton, and Compton Verney have no station at all. It will be useful to go behind this orientation and look at the original distribution of wealth in our area.

This wealth consists in wood and stone and iron and coal and salt, and fish, beasts, and vegetation. The trees of Warwickshire and Worcestershire were once its most prominent feature; when cut down, they supported the inhabitants by being made into brooms and faggots and hoops and wheels. Most of their villages and towns were built of timber, and the great beams, laced with mud and earth and wattle and osier, still stand together at Coventry beside the wreckage of more recent buildings. Later, they made the first ships of the Navy, and often these foresters were commemorated by the wooden effigies for which Herefordshire was known. Much of this great stock was dissipated; salt, for example, is separated only by fire, and until coal could be generally used, the adjacent forests were drawn upon for these furnaces; in 1665 there were 60,000 smiths in the woods above Dudley. Yarranton said of Wyre Forest, once the most prodigious bulk of timber in the county, "In 10,000 acres of coppice there is not 100 ton fit for ship-building. Had the Act of Elizabeth been observed, there would have been at least 40 good oak trees to the acre." Individual enthusiasts (the Foleys, for example) tried to reverse this process, and both James I. and Charles II. attempted to enforce the plantation of mulberry trees, of which that in Shakespeare's garden was probably one, and from which silk might be made. Hardly, however, had the landscape gardeners finished their belted groves and vistas of oak and elm and cedar, when a new demand arose from the enlarged naval estimates of the late eighteenth century. Many landowners were alive to this new responsibility, and the family of Nash the historian, for example, planted 60,000 trees around this time. The Napoleonic wars drew heavily on this area, and such splendid relics as the crescent of elms at Hanley Castle, extending for three-quarters of a mile and dating from 1641, were cut down. In 1804, when it was thought that Napoleon might effect a landing

F

from Boulogne, a committee was set up at Evesham for the cultivation of walnut trees, of which the wood made excellent gun-stocks. Many of these beautiful trees survive, and it is in the lemon-shade of one of them that I write.

This burst of national ardour was characteristically preceded by the discovery of a rare Vergilian tree and followed by an outbreak of specialist planting in which the arboretum was cultivated with all the rude energy of the early nineteenth century. On an oak-laden eminence near Abberley a tree, common near Angers but unknown in the British Isles, had recently resisted the efforts of two landowners to graft it. This was the *sorbus sativa pyriformis*, which has fruit and bark like a pear, leaf and blossom like a mountain ash. Its fruit has a bitter, harsh taste, and in the third Georgic Vergil refers to its use as a stiffener of indifferent wines—

> " et pocula laeti
> Fermento atque acidis imitantur vitea sorbis."

At Arley Park, the Earl of Mountnorris and his son planted, between 1815–20, a large collection of exotic trees, including the American oak, maple, and hickory, and in 1829 a nursery at Worcester offered for sale an astonishing number of trees, among which larch, ash, oak, and fir alone made nearly a million. In contrast to this, Nash reports at Hanley Castle another rare tree, the *sorbus aucuparia*, 43 feet in height and 8 feet clear from ground to branches. This " true service tree " had a very close and firm wood, flowered white in May, and after sixty years gave in the autumn a great many red, yellow, and green berries the size of oranges and tasting like medlars.

The great quarries of Chellaston and Tutbury, in which many enormous and ageless toads lie sightlessly immured, are outside our area, and many of the fine honey-coloured small manor-houses on its southern periphery are of Cotswold stone and thus also ineligible ; but we have local workings. The quarries at Rowington have been worked since 1314, and stone from here was used for St. Philip's, Birmingham. The pretty Georgian bridge at Warwick was built from the Rock Mills at Emscote. Shipston-on-Stour has many excellent eighteenth-century stone houses, and that of Wilmcote was used to pave Barry's Houses of Parliament. The Victoria Quarry near Rugby contains thirty-five bands of limestone, and we have also manganese at Hartshill, gypsum near Alcester,

43   FRIAR STREET, WORCESTER

The North Prospect of St. Philip's Church &c. in Birmingham.

The North Prospect of St. Philip's Square in Birmingham

St. Philip's Church...

BIRMINGHAM

and fuller's-earth at Tachbrook. The excellence of the free-stone in this area can be seen by comparing that used, for example, at Croome Court with the sour brown stones of Blenheim.

The prominence of salt in the medieval budget is an historical fact that we find hard to visualise with any ease. Fish and meat, we know, are better cooked otherwise by immersion for several months in salt; salt as a manure is not now commonly used, and salts as a medicinal instrument are in declining favour. Yet salt was once a fundamental of human life, exchangeable against gold or a lifelong lease, and St. Richard de Burford, a thirteenth-century saint, was for a long time believed by the people of Droitwich to have been elevated because, the springs having once dried up, he had caused them to flow again. These springs (Leland remarks three of them) are known to have been worked in 816, when wood was cut down in their service. By Leland's time 6000 loads were sent away each year. By 1688 the springs, then presumed to be working at capacity, were so profitable that their proprietors attempted to have their position regularised as a monopoly. From this arose one of those ruthless and extended conflicts which, involving many innocent investors and conducted with Italian ferocity, are the commonplace of expanding capitalism. In 1690, a Robert Steynor bought land adjoining that of the existing owners, and spent £6000 in establishing his right to work it. This principle of free entry encouraged so many others that the price was soon cut to a quarter of its normal figure, thus crippling the original holders, for their overhead costs could not be diminished and the goodwill of their trade was largely destroyed. Thus in 1708 they brought in a Bill for the extension of the market, the cost of this to be borne in part by the newcomers. Steynor, though an experienced litigant, was ruined in his turn by the efforts required to throw out this Bill, and all parties were thus prostrated, and the public interest in no way furthered, when in 1725 Sir Richard Lane, a former mayor and M.P. for Worcester, was led by the depth of salt workings in Cheshire to suspect that those at Droitwich might not, in fact, have been fully explored. He therefore ordered the talc floor of the workings to be pierced, whereupon salt shot up through the aperture in such force that two of the workmen were smothered, and in such profusion that not one-tenth of it could be used. The layers previously worked had indeed been only a thin crust ; but the new discoveries made worthless the shares which, being held the surest of securities, had been the refuge of timid investors, the foundation of many charities, and the jointure of innumerable wives.

A stream of waters resembling those of Epsom occurs at Abberton in Worcestershire ; and those of Cheltenham were first discovered in 1716, when pigeons were noticed to feed off the salty residue of certain streams. But those of Droitwich (than which not even the Dead Sea itself is more salt) must come first, and the brine baths of this spa, in which one rolls and bounces but can never sink, are invincibly droll and far excel the normal amusements of a provincial town.

The coal-mines of this area are numerous, but shallow; few accidents or startling discoveries disturb their working. Nuneaton and Chilvers Coton have been worked since Norman times ; sea coal was sold before 1400, and in 1350 a raid was made on Nuneaton Priory for its great stores of coal. This industry also has a history of conflict between private interests, superseded by unexpected but conclusive technical improvement. The Bedworth pits were owned and run until the early seventeenth century by Sir Thomas Beaumont, who employed all his tenants as operatives. One day the pits, always subject to flooding, became inundated, and he abandoned both them and the entire village to rot. From this they were rescued in 1619 by two persons called Bugge and Robinson, who, with the mixed motives of industrial chivalry, proposed to re-open the pits on condition that the price of coal could be kept at double that charged by the neighbouring colliery of Griff. These had, therefore, to be partly bought, partly forced out of business. In 1630 they opened up again and easily undercut Bugge and Robinson, who could find no better way of stopping this than by diverting into their pits the water accumulated by a storm. Later, a series of slumps and instances of inefficiency put the whole area out of action until in 1684 municipal control was established. In the eighteenth century the fifty-five pits then flourishing had the use of new steam engines devised for them by Watt.

While it would be wearisome, and in a book of this size obviously inadequate, to detail the many iron and steel industries contained in the Birmingham area, the history of each of these is the history of the determination of Shake-

speare's people to make something more than a living out
of Shakespeare's country. There has always been (although
it is rash to generalise) a lively contact between employers
and their staffs, elsewhere precluded by the mere size of
factories and organisations. For this reason the Trades
Union Movement did not at first obtain much hold, and the
survey made in 1891 by Sydney and Beatrice Webb showed
that only 4·19 per cent. of workers were affiliated, as against,
for example, 11·23 per cent. in Northumberland. Possibly, however, this is in part because the home-workers, a notoriously
sweated body, were difficult to organise, having little corpo-
rative spirit; moreover, the course of the movement, begun
in 1872 by Joseph Arch, shows how quickly a naïve and
agricultural body, however large its size (and this had 100,000
members in a year), will divide and waste its forces unless it
has methods as ruthless as those it seeks to combat.

This is necessarily an adaptable race, for it has constantly
happened that an industry, developed over many generations
and the support of whole townships, is yet ruined in a few
months by a change of fashion, a technical discovery, or a
remote political move. Even the great woollen industry
subsided in this way, and it had been the heart of Coventry,
making it the fourth town in the kingdom. There was a
season at Coventry in 1638, and in the late eighteenth century
there was often horse-racing outside the town. Wool had
been sent from there (to Leicester, for example) as early as
1254, and in the fourteenth century industrial specialisa-
tion was well advanced both here and in Worcester, where
the names occur of Ironmonger, Baxter, Herringmonger,
Chapman, Spicer, Cobbler, Taylor, Purser, Organer, and
Fysshe. Till about 1400, wool had been sold mostly raw,
and not towns only but the great Cistercian houses of Combe
and Stoneleigh produced it; but by 1445 there were three
score each of drapers, weavers, fullers, and dyers in Coventry.
The ship-money assessment of 1635 shows clearly how the
old alignment of industry persisted long after the Reformation, for Birmingham is assessed at only £160, as against
Coventry's £500, Warwick's £150, and Stratford's £30.

Birmingham is essentially an armoury, and has been one
since Benedict the Cutler set up there under Edward VI.
This, almost alone among human trades, has known no
fluctuation more serious than the restriction of individual

fancy imposed by the army regulation of 1821. Craftsmen who had previously taken pride in meeting every refinement of personal taste had now to conform to a standard pattern. Other trades were dependent on fashion or seasonal needs. William III., for instance, introduced the buckle trade, and the sudden substitution in 1791 of shoe-strings for buckles proved the ruin of twenty thousand persons. Mines were often flooded out ; the miners of Bedworth twice in 1800 made raids on Coventry in such force that a regiment had to be sent to drive them out. In 1789, again, half Birmingham depended on brooches and latchets and watch-chains ; but the French Revolution and the veto imposed by Napoleon on imported luxuries quickly extinguished this trade, despite the gallant efforts of Queen Charlotte, who repeatedly appeared at Court fairly clanking with her apparatus of steel buckles, latchets, and slides. Nor is it agreeable to think of the thirty families who spent all of every year in making nutcrackers, in the hope that gentility or a bumper crop would cause people to weary of cracking nuts between finger and thumb. Those, by contrast, who in the first two decades of Victoria's reign exported to South America gouges, skeleton keys, jacks, tomahawks, manacles, handcuffs, chains for Brazilian slaves, and in one case a regular two dozen of thumbscrews, lived well and need no commiseration.

More delicate uses were found for craftsmanship ; the Soho mastery of cloisonné, champlevé, and encrusted enamelling was the inspiration of much of Pugin's medievalist enthusiasm ; and Boulton's ormolu factory-clocks have still a certain perverse attraction. The late eighteenth century saw such thoughtful novelties as the improvement of the bayonet and the link-up with iron-yards at Swansea ; and it was in 1790 that Birmingham brought forth its first umbrella. Forty years later a wholesale tea and coffee dealer called Cadbury began to experiment with the making of cocoa and chocolate. Currency itself, the blood of commerce, flowed in an ever-widening torrent, not only for home consumption (though of this alone 400 tons a year were produced) but for Russia, Spain, and Mexico ; such frail administrations as the 1859 provisional Tuscan Government bought their pennies from this original store.

Everywhere there are signs of this rage for self-advancement. How many houses in this area have the large top

45 VICTORIA SQUARE : with the Classic Town Hall

46 CHAMBERLAIN PLACE : with the Gothic University

CHAMBERLAIN BIRMINGHAM

47 A FARMYARD, WARNDON, WORCESTERSHIRE

· 48 A MILLPOND, WELFORD-ON-AVON, WARWICKSHIRE

windows needed for weaving ? In Tudor times the blueness
of Coventry thread was famous. The little Arrow was
tapped for mill-wheels. Someone, by taking thought, invented the eye of the needle. And in the midst of all this,
there were such ingenuous unchanging trades as the scythe-
making of Cradley, the nautical chain-making of Netherton,
the shovels of Oldbury. The porcelain of Worcester, started
by people whom the declining cloth trade had ceased to
support, is prized by local collectors ; but the tapestry-maps
of Barcheston are everyone's pride.

Barcheston, a mile south-east of Shipston-on-Stour, lying
in lush country and having a church in whose tower are cells
for two anchorites, is the birthplace of Richard Hyckes, a
weaver who, on returning from the study of his craft in the
Low Countries, was set up in his trade by William Sheldon,
his squire. Sheldon was an excellent squire, and this was
the expanding sixteenth century ; thoughtful for art and for
the wise employment of his villagers, he made over the
greater part of his inheritance in return for an assurance that
the making of " tapestry, arras, moccadoes, carolles, plon-
ketts, groygraynes, says, and serges " would be continued.
Barcheston work included the famous maps and also a number
of remarkable heraldic pieces, in which the quarterings are
varied by the introduction of moral figures—Pride and Sloth,
for example, and Luxury. One of these, dated about 1560,
contains the first known picture of an English turkey, and
shows this bird to be already established in its moral orbit ;
while the representation of Luxury (a man and woman pawing
upon a bench) strikes oddly in this stylised design. Iris and
honeysuckle, apple and cucumber, roses and mallow came
easily to men working in Warwickshire, and the same affec-
tionate observation comes out in the county maps, for these
cover only a few days' marching from Barcheston. In the
early seventeenth century, however, new allegorical schemes
appear, with nothing in them of heraldry or of the drabness
of Elizabethan wallpapers. One of these is the series of
" The Seasons," now at Hatfield. Each of these must be read
as carefully as a battle-piece of Uccello, for around the central
figure there is in each panel a multiplicity of incident, carried
on simultaneously in several perspectives, and allowing, for
example, of fish inset upon a winter sky. It is curious to
notice that the hills in the Spring panel, though similar in their

context to those in a valley-scene of Patinir, must in fact be taken from the Blue Cotswolds, a little way from Barcheston.

The workmen of Barcheston are an exception to one of our rules, for it is almost certain that for a time they removed to the ateliers of Mortlake in order to escape the danger in which, as the protégés of a great Cavalier family, they naturally stood. But warfare was not at that time so far advanced as to call for a scorched-earth policy against the invader, and the troops from London could breathe in the harvest air; for this is an area in which husbandry has known no interval. Visited by no locust-cloud, rigid in no permanent frost, hissing with no tropical vapours, the area is just such an equable paradise as the Sardinian forests or the vineyards by the Yonne. The intensity of its present culture can have had no parallel since the time of the Napoleonic wars, and yet it remains " of subtle, tender, and delicate temperance," driving its green harbingers to the very gates of industry.

Cobbett, remarking the nice adjustment of industry with agriculture in this area, said that one of its largest manufactures, that of gloves, was carried on mostly in people's houses, singly and within sight of the " fields and hop-gardens where the husband and sons must live in order to raise the food and drink and wool." " That is a great thing," he said, " for the land." The wool trade, for all its wealth, was not helpful to agriculture, and even the monastic houses deserted this primary care for the obsessing fleece. The two-fifths of land which remained arable went on a three-year rotation; wheat or rye, barley, oats, beans, or pease, and a fallow year; this cycle went round without variation until in the early seventeenth century turnips and artificial grasses were introduced from the Low Countries. But the meat and corn became more profitable than wool, and the fattest sheep less welcome than those Hereford cattle whose white faces and dark red bodies Cobbett thought the finest he had seen. But on Arthur Young's visitation in 1768 there was still little change; turnips and barley and wheat went round, with nothing new in the earth but clover. It was during the French wars that potatoes and cabbages and carrots came in, and a fleece still came to three pounds of wool. Meanwhile, an observer might have looked down upon the unchanging fields from one of many of the great trees which, whether neatly in parks or casually by the way, make these the timber counties ; such a watcher would see sometimes a novelty, the maze of hornbeam at Hewell Grange, for instance, or the iron palisades of Woodnorton behind which the Duc d'Orleans enclosed wild boar and Australian bustard, and sometimes such a hostage to the future as the sale of twenty fourteenth-century oaks from Kyre Park to make dock-gates (45 feet by 24 feet) for Grimsby.

The early Hanoverian period was one of great evolution, and hardly a year passed without some new amenity ; in 1764 Joseph Elkington of Princethorpe invented a scheme of under-drainage, by which auger-holes were let down to the underlying water, and for this received £1000 from Parliament ; two years later a new interest in livestock was aroused by the display at Worcester of the celebrated Lincolnshire black ox. This animal, which had been shown " twice in one week " to the Royal Family, weighed 243 stones and " much resembled an elephant in the hinderparts " excited the liveliest comment at the " public tea drinkings " which, held at four o'clock and accompanied by music, were the rage of the time. Seven years later a pig was sold at Astbury and found to weigh 1084 pounds and to measure 10 feet round and 10 feet long. Between 1763–66 great resentment was caused by a tax on cider, for this trade was then at its height ; but for all the furious campaign, the firework displays, and the ox roasted under the sky, little trouble was taken to improve the orchards from which this wealth was drawn. Pomeroy the topographer remarks how little they were tended, how trees were crowded together, molested by cattle, and left to decay. Gardeners were more concerned with novelties, with the Royal African Strawberry from Tangier, the large-leaved African Endive, and the Large Prolific Antwerp Yellow Raspberry ; while to Bath and Bristol there was a roaring trade in Battersea Asparagus.

In the nineteenth century a new earnestness can be detected in every department of life ; ultimate problems were raised, and the Chartists and the National Land Company made practical experiments in our area. Land was bought, and mechanics and industrial workers enticed from their benches and lathes. Only the national taste for strawberries saved the Company from immediate destruction, and there are other schemes which recall Bakunin or the agricultural enterprise in *Virgin Soil*. Ruskin, for example, was in 1877 given twenty acres of ground on the edge of Wyre forest by the Mayor of Birmingham, and on it established several families in the hope that they would be self-supporting and even, by barter, attain a high standard of existence. But in general the employers had the better of this century, and the great natural wealth of the area, combined with the improvements of the time and the innocence of unorganised labour, made this a profitable era ; not, indeed, till plum orchards were sold to ex-servicemen in 1920 at £200 an acre was there such an opening for opportunism.

Much of the information in this chapter has been found in Mr. R. C. Gaut's compilation, *A History of Worcestershire Agriculture and Rural Evolution*.[1] This remarkable work is disappointing only in its conclusions. I should have thought, for example, that for the penultimate paragraph of a study of some 200,000 words some more stimulating sentence could have been found than this : " in wet weather the farmer dons the gum-boot for footwear." Fortunately we have no need of books for our postscript ; the reader has only to take his eye from the page and run it instead across the landscape seen through the papered panel of the carriage window. It is not simply that this landscape is packed and stuffed as if each handful of earth had been carried by hand, as if this were an island gifted by nature with nothing but thistle and scrub. It is not simply that indoors as well, in many great empty houses, the carpets are up and the curtains down and the ceiling never so high that there would be room for another sack of sugar-beet seed. It is that this country is once again campaigning country, up in arms as it was three hundred years ago. There is not, perhaps, very much to learn from the strategy of the civil wars ; Liddell Hart and Hugh Slater could draw no moral from the siege of Worcester (although it would be a possible exercise, around the hill-town of Warwick, to reconstruct the successful action of de Gaulle at Laon). So much of the necessity of war is disagreeable that one could dwell endlessly upon the new richness of this area, calling to mind the barges hooting to one another at night on the Severn, the fat acres of Evesham and the orderlies parading in the double cube, the aeroplane glimpsed like a leopard in the park, and the Italian prisoner singing in the field.

[1] Littlebury & Co., Worcester, 1939. 15s. net.

49   FARMING PROSPECT AT PENDOCK, ON THE SEVERN-AVON PLAIN

50 GRIMSHAW HALL, KNOWLE, WARWICKSHIRE

IV

HOUSES AND SOME PEOPLE

HOUSES may not be considered apart from people, and the temper of this people has been defined as inventive, meddlesome, and sanguine. Not all, of course, are as inventive as Murdock ; nor all as meddlesome as that William de Beauchamp who supported Queen Maud against King Stephen and in consequence forfeited all his estate ; and very few have been as sanguine as that Nicholas Lechmere who, when introduced into the House of Commons, did not so much as take his seat before bursting incontinently into a harangue. Nevertheless these are recurring traits, and it would be amusing to see how far they have found expression in the domestic architecture of the area.

Let us say, in paradox, that no man has a house more personal to himself than he who chooses to have none ; but if priests and beggars and hermits enjoy this last refinement of caprice, so also do those—witches, for example, and fugitives—who might wish themselves to have a roof, but are yet forced to do without one. We have examples of all these extremities ; the most famous of our hermits is probably Guy of Guy's Cliffe, an early example of the picaresque hero, but one unhappily not found in any chronicle and so thickly dusted over with tourist sentiment as to be less vivid than many of the other figures (Ruskin, *e.g.*, and Mrs. Siddons) with whom the house itself is coupled. A more curious hermit is the historian Lazamon, who lived for many years on the boundaries of Astley and Arley, sitting where an arrangement of rocks set the whole Severn foaming, and persuaded travellers to offer alms in propitiation ; from this traffic he was able to write his *History of England from Brute to Cadwallader*, and dedicated to Queen Eleanor the lifetime's work represented by this short traverse.

Witches and wizards were equally common; in 1323 John de Nottingham was hanged near Coventry for sticking pins into images of public figures, and pride in the orthodoxy of this early example must mingle with pleasure at the fantasy of later ones—that, among others, of Widow Robinson, her two daughters, and an undefined man. This clique was arraigned in 1660 and claimed, not merely to be able to unseat the monarchy, but to be capable also of a far more uncommon feat—the transformation of corn into pepper. Fifty years later, near Kidderminster, a Mrs. Hicks was hanged, and she, having first caused her neighbours to vomit pins, had later become ambitious of raising a storm from the elements by removing her stockings in public and making a lather with soap. Among such complicated devices it is comforting to come upon one whose skill was in dialectic : in 1649 a witch was hanged at Worcester, a witch whose obstinate skill in argument was the terror of her examiners ; and the name of this witch was Rebecca West.

Almost as indestructible as the fact of having had no house at all is the fact of having had a castle. Even now there is something as permanent as poetry or those sounds which, once made, can never be quite lost to hearing, in the idea of a castle, and from these lines written at Sissinghurst :

> " This husbandry, this castle, and this I
> Moving within the deeps,
> Shall be content within our timeless spell
> Assembled fragments of an age gone by,"

we are won to sympathy even with such a creation as faces us on the road from Tewkesbury to Ledbury. Eastnor Castle was designed in the style of Edward I. by Sir Robert Smirke, a pupil of Soane, and most easily kept in mind by reference to the British Museum, which he completed in 1847. Smirke was a ready hand at Castle Gothic, and, when not sitting on the Committee of Taste or perfecting his Hellenic manner by cautious Mediterranean travel, would design private and public buildings alike in this Highland style. Thus it is less to Maxstoke or Kenilworth than to the Council Buildings of Carlisle (designed by Smirke in 1811) that this castle recalls us. Of the authentic fortresses, Kenilworth, Maxstoke, and Warwick would detain us longer if they had not been so often and so learnedly considered, to the neglect of later work. The case of Kenilworth (10) is curious in that the long, ragged, and not pretty village is for the most part a consequence of the overwhelming influence of Scott, but at Sudeley, at the south-western rim of the area, there is a later and subtler association. Sudeley, like Kenilworth, was largely demolished during the Civil War, but in the year of Queen Victoria's coronation it came under new ownership and was most skilfully, almost preciously restored, until to-day the surviving fourteenth-century tower and the great looping fenestration of the broken wing have that quality which makes one prefer their fragments to any imaginable whole. The outbuildings of Sudeley are likewise reflected in water and buttressed with flowers, until there is one corner which might have supplied the image used of a young invalid by Henry James : " his serenity was but the array of wild flowers niched in his ruin." Yet Maxstoke also has much of this composure ; this house, being keepless and from its origin fulfilling a domestic, rather than a martial, purpose, has little, in the double stillness imposed on it and its reflected image by its wide encircling moat, of the arbitrary passion implied in the notion of a castle. To the west, for instance, there is a great window with elaborate Perpendicular tracery very different from the embattled winking of windows made for defence ; and though the gatehouse has two high commanding turrets, the way beneath it is vaulted and groined, the bosses carved as if for peace, and the moat (according to Henry VIII.'s commissioners) is remarkable more for its wealth of fish than for any defensive engines.

Contemplation of castles, with their terrible reduction of life to the single purpose of survival, their mimicry of nature's fortress, the conical hill, and their stubborn beauty in decay, may easily deceive us into forgetting how primitive were the principles of building involved. Such cottages as survive from this period show that only the use of stone, and perhaps the greater pace of military evolution—the influence, on one view, of Syrian, on another of French examples—raises these houses of war above the hutches which were thought enough for peace. Brickwork, of which the Romans had brought a very tolerable knowledge, had been neglected by the Saxons, and was re-introduced largely by those nobles who, while in France during the Hundred Years' War, had been envious of those chateaux whose example was followed at Tattershall and Hurstmonceux ; building was thus necessarily of wood and mud and wattle and plaster, and for a long time the type of private house was very like

> " Tea-Pot Hall
> All roof, no wall."

The use of horizontals for making upright walls and lifting the roof-structure to head-level was a long time coming, for builders at this time were very conservative ; but at Didbrook and Tirley, in the south-west corner of our area, are two excellent examples : the one is a cottage in which the roof timbers are first raised from the inclined crucks and then

[*Drawn by Sydney R. Jones*]

51   LOWER BROCKHAMPTON, NEAR BROMYARD

braced apart by horizontal rafters ; and at Tirley there is a barn in which, though wall and roof form a single curve, there is nevertheless an attempt to break away from the inverted V which, whatever its topical interest for ourselves, was a very limited and awkward shape in which to live. Later, the use of posts and wall-plates made possible the erection of box-shaped houses, in addition to the inverted-dinghy mode already available, and this, with its single interior room, was the type of the medieval manor. At Lower Brockhampton, near Bromyard, there is a late fourteenth-century manor, with gatehouse and moat, much prized by connoisseurs of this barbarous style (51, 56). It is curious in that it has the gatehouse, a feature also of the castle-plan and an essential of fortification ; this gatehouse is of two

52 MAXSTOKE CASTLE FROM THE AIR

53 HALF-TIMBER AT EARL'S CROOME

54 THE OLD VICARAGE, ASHLEWORTH, NEAR THE SEVERN

55 MERE HALL, DROITWICH

storeys, the upper projecting on curved brackets sprung from the moulded heads of the angle-posts; it has an arched entrance, north and south, with an interior wicket, and is an admirable piece of unfussy building. The manor itself is almost a century older than the gatehouse, and its roof, with its central tie-beam, curved braces, diagonal queen-posts and collar (56)—the excellent composition of this group, an epitome at once of the military arrangement of medieval domestic building and the approaching magnificence of Tudor seats, may not be called wholly deliberate. Yet the house, with its single hall of two main bays and screen-bay at the east end, its exposed timber-framing with alternation

[Drawn by Sydney R. Jones

56 THE HALL, LOWER BROCKHAMPTON

of close-set and large square panels, can stand very well for the small half-timbered manor. At Bosbury, not far from Brockhampton, the remnants of Old Court farm, once a manor-house of the Bishops of Hereford, show this style of building at a slightly higher level; the gatehouse, for instance, has an outer wall of irregular stone blocks, and a major and minor archway whose rearing arches display that interaction of civil and ecclesiastical style which is integral to medieval building, but is thought immoral when used (by Adam, for instance) to vary the slavish conformity of later centuries.

Most pre-Renaissance building in this area is half-timber building, and Habershon, whose *Half-Timbered Houses of England* appeared in 1836, records that even a hundred years ago very few of these surviving houses were of earlier date than 1500. This, in fact, is one of many cases in which antiquity in itself is no virtue, for it is a style which becomes of surpassing interest only at a relatively advanced stage of its evolution. This stage is marked by the retention of many early features, such as the gatehouse—which at Westwood (71) and Charlecote is a creation of the greatest dignity and elaboration—or the use of a single main hall (Nash remarks, at Arley Hall, near Stourport, the great hall now cut up into sitting-rooms with dais, on the lines of a college at the elder universities), or the modified fortification, the moat, and turreted point of vantage ; but the sum of these was the manor-house of the great period (1550–1640) of English vernacular, the style of Mere Hall, Salwarpe Court, Elmley Lovet, and Woolas Hall.

Habershon mentions few houses of earlier date than 1500, and says, in fact, " it is almost impossible to find a house, not of the order of castles, the principal apartments of which are older than the reign of Henry VII." The latest example he gives is Elmley Lovet, of which the central gable bears the date 1635 ; this he holds an exceptionally late instance of authentic half-timbered vernacular, and one whose details already display Italian influence. Within this period half-timbering had time to find in itself a domestic medium of the greatest charm and convenience, living off no predecessor, able by an aggregation of gables and a nice alternation of structural with decorative motifs, at once to look spontaneous and to fulfil the increasing demands of a newly affluent class. Some of these houses were partly of stone, and very few differed in essentials from the hall with solar and servants' quarters seen at Little Wolford Manor (part of which is of the fourteenth century). This forerunner of Harvington, Huddington, and Baddesley Clinton lies on the southern periphery of the area, near Shipston-on-Stour, and for all its pearly Cotswold stone, Renaissance detail, and squared

57   HUDDINGTON COURT, WORCESTERSHIRE: Before restoration

[*Drawn by W. Curtis Green, R.A.*]

windows it is, with its steep tiled roof and single projecting and battlemented eminence, the nucleus of these later houses in which Papists lay hid; even to-day a house entirely in this medium, conspicuous as a zebra among the greens of the orchard country and the brown of the arable, is as grateful to the traveller's eye as the uprooted signpost. In the open country they blend most happily; dazzling in snow, flaky and aromatic in the heat of summer, there is no season at which this necessitous manner of building does not strike happily upon the eye. Yet it is equally suited to towns, not simply in its humbler guise (although Cropthorne, Norton (9), and Ombersley (30) deserve their reputation) but also in those more ample, even brilliant, examples whose present function of hotel or public house so greatly increases the pleasure of inspecting them. Few towns are without one such, but Ledbury and Tewkesbury must have between them a dozen, and the St. Katherine's Hospital at Ledbury shows also how easily it may be adapted to special needs; the area also has several examples of half-timbering in church architecture. Nor is it necessarily black-and-white; not simply may the plaster be colour-washed and the timber a natural brown, but the interstices may be filled with brick. It may also (as at Preston Court, near Ledbury) be faced with a rough stucco. Apperley Hall, in the orchard country below Tewkesbury, is an enchanting example of this compromise, which is, moreover, safe from the subsidence common among wood-and-plaster work. It was found also at a house whose restoration is more than usually to be deplored—at Huddington; early photographs and drawings of this house show that its panelling was alternately of brick and plaster, each weathered and without artificial colour, each distinguished from the others by some variation of height or breadth (57). In place of this is now a uniform Trust House black-and-white, walls being broken and extra gables inserted in existing bays. The house is, however, of the greatest human interest as being, perhaps, among many Worcestershire houses, that most implicated in the Gunpowder Plot.

This Plot is characteristic of a century in which, in almost all disputes, a certain moral dignity may be credited to both sides. Thus the conspirators were not ambitious brutes, but honourable men of high standing in the county; nor was their scheme originally one of blood and violence; but

58, 59 CHESTERTON, WARWICKSHIRE, THE HILL AND THE MILL

60 COMPTON WYNYATES, WARWICKSHIRE

DISSIMILAR NEIGHBOURS OF THE HILL COUNTRY

61 THE GREAT CHAMBER, WESTWOOD HOUSE

the end, in this case, could be attained only by means remote
from those envisaged by the company at its foundation.
The Shakespeare country has always been a country of dissent,
and many examples, some of greater intellectual, some of
greater historical, interest will occur in these pages ; but
there can be none so dramatic as this one, and the bloody,
belated, incompetent ride of the fugitives is, in itself, a survey
of our area, starting as it did at Rugby, moving through
Warwick to Huddington, on without pause to Tardebigge,
Burcot, Lickey End, Clent, and Hagley, breaking up at
Holbeach and going to earth at Hindlip, or in the woods, or
over the border in Shropshire. Unhappily none of the houses
— Huddington, Hindlip, Coughton, Grafton — has escaped
restoration, and each in consequence is exceeded in architectural interest by houses of less historical importance—
Mere, Salwarpe, Harvington, and Ashleworth. Hindlip,
however, and for all that it is now entirely altered, deserves
record as one of the most foxy houses imaginable—fitted out,
in fact, as a refuge by Thomas Habington, whose hobby and
secondary employment this was. It had been built about
1572 by his father, John Habington, who was cofferer to
Queen Elizabeth and the husband of one of her ladies ; Thomas
Habington, once sequestrated in Worcestershire, began to
equip his house in the service of those many whose religion
was not in favour at the time, and in 1605 this enterprise was
put to the test. Every precaution had been taken against a
long siege ; each asylum, whether reached through a closet,
by a hole in the chimneys, or down a concealed trap, was
ventilated by a system of funnels. To not all of the eleven,
however, could food be brought ; and in none was there
provision against those natural necessities which confinement
serves to emphasise. Thus two of the plotters had to give
up after four days, having subsisted for that time upon a
single apple. In the chimney, however, was the most subtle
of all his contrivances, and in this Henry Garnett, a Jesuit
remarkable even in this seventeenth century for learning and
authority, resisted eight days of search. The entrance to his
hole was bricked up, covered with panelling, and hardly
distinguishable from the rest of the chimney-piece ; and in
it Garnett and another Jesuit were fed, by way of a second
chimney-shaft, with cawdles, broth, marmalade, and sweet-
meats ; and between these rather sickly meals they were

provided with the "books, massing stuff, and popish trumpery" remarked by their pursuers. On the eighth day they could no longer support the atmosphere, and, giving themselves up, were presently hanged in St. Paul's churchyard. Garnett was a man of European reputation ; Addison, for example, noticed a portrait of him at Loretto, and in 1610 a Cretan Jesuit called Eudaemo Johannes published an apology for him ; privy to, but not active in, the Gunpowder Plot, he had come to England after succeeding Clavius as professor of Hebrew and philosophy at the Italian College of Rome.

Baddesley Clinton, almost alone among these recusant manors, preserves its architectual interest whole ; this enchanting fifteenth-century house, moated, built in turns of brick and stone and half-timber, with its massive gatehouse tower looking back to the Edwardian, looking forward to the Elizabethan, with its tall and moulded but undecorated chimneys and square-built fenestration, recalls the castle-plan also in being built about three sides of a quadrangle, and enclosing a garden. Entrance is across a brick bridge of the early eighteenth century, and the house, for the most of grey sandstone, stands in one of the originals of those great parks for which Warwickshire is remarkable ; the outer oak door (and never can an oak have been sported more impregnably) with its wicket and hinges as big as a leg of beef, is attributed to the middle fifteenth century, and much of the interior woodwork and furniture is as good as anyone could wish. Fugitives are said to have been concealed here in a room beneath the moat—a phrase almost intolerably mysterious and exciting to those who have read *The Prisoner of Zenda* at a sufficiently early age. Harvington also has a tradition of this kind, but is properly a stone house of the seventeenth century and later, and to complete our list of half-timbered houses it is better to consider some whose connotation is wholly peaceful.

At Ashleworth, in the Gloucestershire fragment of the area, there is an E-shaped manor of two storeys and attic, whose second storey and gables project appreciably above the first, giving to the whole an air of squatting which would be droll if it were not for the beautiful proportioning of this house, which, with its nicely-weighted upper and lower windows and arrangement of horizontal, vertical, and diagonal

62   THE ENTRANCE FRONT, EASTINGTON HALL, LONGDEN, WORCESTERSHIRE

From a Water-Colour
by A. Troyte Griffith

lines, is a ravishing piece of English vernacular (54). At Earls Croome there is a house of three storeys, whose peculiar virtue is in its relation to the great trees which approach it ; for its regular front and almost finicky timbering seem to anticipate the *architecture chiffrée* of 150 years later (53). Such order is not in the half-timber tradition, for this is essentially a wayward medium, made for second thoughts ; Salwarpe Court, for instance, birthplace in 1381 of Richard Beauchamp, is an irregular old house, thought by Habershon to have been " much larger than it is at present " (i.e. *c.* 1830) and distinguished by the elegant barge-boards upon the sixteenth-century addition in its middle (63). Little Grimshaw Hall is a second irregular masterpiece (50).

The most brilliant, however, of all half-timbered houses in the area lies close to Droitwich, and in the parish of Hanbury. Mere Hall, though dated 1337, is mostly of the sixteenth century. Between the two great flanking gables are five subsidiary ones, built above an unbroken line of fenestration, itself surmounting a central mass of which the boarding, and the pedimented barley-sugar porch, achieve an effect of wit necessarily uncommon in this medium (55). The variety of this central section is played off against the roof-line of the gables at each end, for this extends unbroken from the top of the house (hardly surmounted even by the Elizabethan chimneys) almost to the ground, and against the octagonal turret or cupola which crowns the middle of the five minor gables. This house was much altered by Habershon, whose wide knowledge of the medium persuaded him to employ carpenters' Gothic fenestration in place of that shown in earlier prints ; but it is in the neighbouring village of Hadzor that his work is shown to full advantage, for this, being wholly of half-timber and in some state of decay, was restored by him during his employment at the Hall.

Birtsmorton Court, though somewhat extensively rebuilt in 1920 after a fire, can very well sum up for this period of English building, for it also is moated, reached by a bridge, protected by an immense gateway, and itself built round an open court. Yet it is neither for this, nor even for the excellent wainscoted interior, that it is most interesting ; for the one we have seen already, and no interior of this period in our area can compare with, say, that at Levens Hall, which is a late Elizabethan example of extraordinary luxuriance, and

augmented by such curiosities as the clasp from Napoleon's
cloak and a set of china from Sèvres, ornamented with a
scene of the Emperor hunting and formerly the property
of Wellington. Birtsmorton is a prize in that it unites in
its personal associations those characteristics of adventure,
conscience, and response to changing conditions which we
have remarked in the people of this area. Thus it was the
refuge of Lord Cobham, prominent among those Lollards
whose recusancy is so much in place in Worcestershire ; it
was the home of the Hakluyts ; and it was the birthplace in
1760 of William Huskisson, a young man whose fortune it
was to be in Paris at the fall of the Bastille and to become the
first of the " new men " of English politics, a statesman seen
to no advantage in society or on the election platform, but
in his administrative skill and knowledge of affairs earning
the admiration even of those, like Lord Melbourne, who
were personally least in sympathy with him. Huskisson, an
initiator to the last, was the first man in England to be killed
by a train, and even Greville in his *Diary* had a word of regret
for him.

This is not an area of gigantic houses, and those so far
described would not, all put together, be as large as that
famous congeries near Sevenoaks which pride of lineage and
natural eloquence have recently made familiar to many
readers. We have seen no seven-acre houses, and only one
above whose park there is always a line of stationary gogglers.
This is Compton Wynyates (60) ; and the great trees of the
Shakespeare country, which elsewhere form avenues, as at
Mere and Coughton, or fill surrounding parks, as at Charlecote
and Hanbury, for the embellishing of great houses, here rise
up and around and above until the house is seen as if in the
bowl of an enormous spoon. Vineyards stood formerly upon
the sides of this hill, and the battlements which still run partly
round the house were augmented by a moat. The house is
in plan an aggregate, proceeding from the central hall to
such other apartments as came to mind, and it is remarkable
for the great beauty of its brickwork and the many felicities
which time was bringing to this disorderly way of building ;
the interior especially is full of small pointers, for not only
is the panelling elaborate and full of such novelties as reversed
clapboarding, but the ceilings represent a reaction from the
exuberant filling-in of much Tudor work and are made,

64 MOAT FARM, DORMSTON

63 SALWARPE COURT

65   THE ENTRANCE FRONT

66   THE STAIRCASE HALL: with its trophies and Thornhill's frescoes

HANBURY HALL, DROITWICH

for instance, of plain, thin boarding tongued and grooved, divided into panels by applied moulded strips, and when plaster is employed it is not in the deep relief and prominent detail of much contemporary work, but with geometrical panels enclosing strapwork ornament in very low relief ; and the rosettes, pellets, and pyramids enclosed in these, if characterless and insipid in themselves, acquire a certain dignity and interest by virtue of their wide spacing. A few years later the Jacobean plasterwork at Aston Hall, though congested and unable to sustain itself over great expanses except by repetition, is clearly evolving into something considerable ; yet for the moment such humbler work as that at Birtsmorton (attributed to Francis Smallman, whose work is found also at Wilderhope, Wenlock Edge, in Shropshire) is more satisfying. An Elizabethan wallpaper exists at Besford, but it has the worst decorative faults of poor plasterwork of this period and is of little interest ; indeed there is little of the imaginative quality of such Jacobean work as exists at Montacute, for instance, in which successive scenes of narrative are shown on a single panel ; and I should leap forward to the work to be seen at Westwood, if it were not that intervening is the frontier formed in architectural history by the Civil War. On the near side of this, however, lies Charlecote (17). Charlecote differs from Compton Wynyates in being demonstrably the work of a single man. John of Padua, architect to Henry VIII. and Edward VI., may not be judged entirely by this house, which has been much done-up, but the gatehouse, equal to that even of Westwood, is a delightful creation, and the turrets, which give to so much Tudor building the air of pavilions, make very welcome this survival of medieval practice, even as is the long gallery, itself of Edwardian origin, a charming irrelevance in many houses of the eighteenth century. Charlecote park is almost the finest of all those in the county, and no earth can look so fine as that which, formerly beneath a layer of ancient turf, is now turned to the production of food. This is also the site of one of the most trivial of Shakespearian legends, and Benjamin Haydon, walking out from Stratford one morning in 1828, struck a more agreeable note : " trees, gigantic and umbrageous, at once announced the growth of centuries, and going close to the waterside I came at once on two enormous old willows, with a large branch aslant the stream, such as Ophelia clung to."

Aston Hall, completed seven years before the outbreak of
war, must also be considered, as a repository of the full Jacobean
style; these two pronounced wings, the numerous Dutch
gables and cupolas, the plain but heavy mullions (67), were
all very soon to disappear, and in the disposition of the hall,
entered in the middle of one side rather than through screens
at each end, the house at last emerges from the fundamental
medieval plan and anticipates a device of the transitional
architect, Smithson, by which the hall becomes more of a
passage and less the great living-room, dividing masters from
servants and bedrooms from kitchen.

[*Drawn by W. Niven*

67   ASTON HALL, BIRMINGHAM

The area has also several excellent Jacobean stone manors,
of which Stanway,[1] a house of extraordinary grace and
amenity, is best known; Woolas Hall (68), however, which
has in its great hall a screen and musicians' gallery like those
of the Middle Temple, is uncommonly fine; and on the
Evesham–Stratford road, Salford Hall is as good as either (18A).
It is, moreover, in the tradition of houses of refuge, for between
1808–30 it was a home for those Benedictine nuns who had
fled from the revolutionary régime in France. It was, moreover, a nest of Popery in the seventeenth century, and had
that rarity of design (revived, however, by Lutyens at Campion
Hall, Oxford), the upstairs chapel. It has the broken elevation of all good minor Jacobean houses; from the farmyard

---

[1] Stanway is in effect a highly sophisticated design, incorporating within a
framework drawn from the monastic plan such features as the Tudor gatehouse, Dutch gables, and the near-classical finials and parapets.

one can make out seven levels of roof, and the interior also is full of refinements not altogether to be presumed in a house so obviously built for work and not for pleasure. The doorway from hall to dining-room, for instance, is Palladian ; each of the main rooms is panelled to the height (12 feet) of its ceiling, and one has an elaborate oak mantelpiece with caryat-

[*Drawn by W. Curtis Green, R.A*.

68   WOOLAS HALL, ON BREDON HILL

ides ; the staircase also is monumental, built into a projection upon the inner court and made of solid blocks of oak, 51 inches in width. Best of all, perhaps, is the roof gallery, which reproduces in more thrifty houses the Long Gallery of the time ; this at Salford is 25 yards in length.

The volumes entitled *Vitruvius Britannicus*, and published between 1715–25 by Colin Campbell under the supervision of Lord Burlington, are a very poor guide to the work they illustrate, for not only do they eliminate innumerable small

I

errors in the building of the seventeenth century, but they minimise the Dutch, and antedate the Italian, influence. In few cases were architects able to move at a bound from the loose aggregation of Gothic to the reasoned formality of Renaissance building, and such distinguished contemporaries of Wren as Talman, Wynne, and Vanbrugh himself were Dutchmen. Campbell has done great harm, not only in rubbing out those irregularities which are the charm of most minor Renaissance houses in England, but in putting about the Jones myth. Inigo Jones, though a designer of extreme originality and a remarkable theorist, was properly a theatrical painter, and the whole trend of Restoration architecture is better understood by reading such a work as the *Notes as to Building Country Houses*, published in 1660 by Sir Roger Pratt, an associate of Jones and the architect of Coleshill. The Jones myth persists at Chesterton and Barton-on-the-Heath, in South Warwickshire ; at Chesterton there is a gazebo transformed into a windmill (59), and the ease and beauty of this design (a difficult exercise in spacing and proportion) make it quite unnecessary to introduce a name for which there is little evidence ; at Barton, by contrast, the manor-house is a very pretty building in brick, with stone cornices, the line of the gables picked out with parapets very like those at Stanway, and the general H-shape combining symmetry with convenience. It is a very well-bred and not in the least a provincial house, but there are many houses of this period which, given the difference between local and metropolitan design, are quite as good. Ilmington Manor, for example, is a plain three-gabled house without the projecting wings of an H but yielding nothing in the nice adjustment of its roofs and the thoughtful asymmetry of door and windows ; and Bredons Norton Manor, of perhaps forty years earlier (1585) is a more complex design, three projecting gables and two recessed, drawn perhaps from half-timbered practice (just as the five small central gables of Mere Hall are reflected in the eleven decorative ones of Pipe Hayes House at Erdington) and possibly rather awkward ; but both of these can stand up to Barton. The house most truly reflecting Inigo Jones is indeed probably Highnam, erected during the interregnum by Carter, a pupil of Jones and surveyor to Oliver Cromwell ; this has since been lived in, but not seriously altered, by Gambier Parry.

69   THE ENTRANCE FRONT AND PERRON, HAGLEY

This area is thick with such charming minor houses as these; let us turn to one of the greater ones which, founded amid the generosity of the Elizabethan Age, was extended at the Restoration " in the style of the Château de Madrid near Paris " (61, 71). Its 208 acres of park extend in rays from the eminence upon which this remarkable house is placed, and it is reached through a gatehouse which is contemporary with the original building and has, as against the solidity and lingering sternness of Charlecote gatehouse, an almost flippant elaboration of detail. The exposed position of the house, and its subsidiary function as " lodge and banqueting-house " to the Pakington family, whose principal seat was at Hampton Lovett, made it at once necessary and easy for it to have, from all angles, a uniformly imposing aspect. The original house was therefore built on a square; and the gardens, with their turrets, pavilions, and ornamental waters, were likewise laid out so that the eye, from whatever angle it chose to survey the scene, was met by what Nash called " a picture of ancient magnificence unequalled by anything in this county." Hampton Lovett was destroyed by fire at the time of the Rebellion, and Westwood was enlarged by the addition of four wings set diagonally upon the house, an arrangement offering certain problems of communication but preserving its original even grandeur. The Corinthian portico, though rather slight for the dimensions of the house, is very pretty and is surmounted by a fine dashing cartouche, on which appears the elephant motif found also in the plaster of the interior; the motif of stars, which gives to the gatehouse its cocky, exuberant air, recurs all round the top of the house, immediately beneath the Dutch gables and the four pyramidal slate-roofed corner-pieces; the alignment of the chimneys is also very subtle, combining the deliberate grouping of the Renaissance with the great height of Tudor chimneys, thus preventing the four pyramids from dwarfing the central section of the house.

Westwood is moreover as good inside as out. The staircase, running narrowly backwards and forwards across the whole width of the house, is not only excellent in itself but has a balustrade of tall Corinthian columns of oak, surmounted by huge balls; it is a most beautiful affair, and superior even to that in the Commandery at Worcester. Many of the later doors leading away from it are as massive and

heavy with ornament as those in the City churches of which
they are contemporaries, and the staircase is finally enriched
by a landscape of Wilson. Upstairs are three rooms containing what is probably the best Restoration plasterwork in
England. Of these the salon is the largest (61), and is filled
in deep relief, set above a frieze of woodwork similarly in
heavy relief and dating from a few years earlier ; this woodwork is relieved by a series of winged but squatting figures,
these the only touch of fantasy in a room which, though
sometimes rebuked for heaviness, is on the contrary a masterpiece of orderly detail, in which many individual panels (those
especially of the ceiling roses) and the alternation of deep
moulding with fine craftsmen-work are entirely satisfying.
The two smaller White and Japanese rooms are by another
hand, and contain, in the one case, a very delicate, and French
rather than English, succession of trees in flower—vine, orange,
lemon, and plum ; in the other a central oval panel, with a
long stem about which fruit, flowers, and foliage are grouped
with a discretion and an individual skill which Miss Jourdain,
for instance, prefers to the later school of Grinling Gibbons,
and secondly a number of heraldic devices, including the tiny
elephant so welcome in this vegetable universe. Westwood
has also an excellent Chinese wallpaper, in which a continuous
motif of flowers extends without repetition for the whole
circuit of the room. This house, on the site of whose kitchen-
garden was originally a Benedictine nunnery, was later a
refuge for dissenters and fugitives from the House of Orange.
Bishops Morley, Fell, and Gunning were received, and in
1660 Dr. Hammond actually died in the house ; and Dean
Hickes, who wrote there his *Linguarum Septentrionalium
Thesaurus*, composed a famous encomium in Latin upon the
house.

It would be impossible to include every good minor
house of the seventeenth and eighteenth centuries, for few
villages have not one of these, and their interest is not cate-
gorical ; rather are there innumerable sorts of penetration
between one style and another, and many houses, though
tricked out with the tall dormers and grouped chimneys and
even the cupola of fashion, are in fact simply brick-built
versions of such half-timbered styles as that of the moat farm
at Dormston (64), to the north-east of Worcester ; this building uses its gables much as a later age uses its dormers, and

the broken parapet and the generally stepped-up air of the house, with its interest pushed as near the roof as possible, may be interpreted as proof either of the many uses of half-timber, or of the true conservatism of later houses.

Besides those houses which, like Croome and Hanbury, are creations of the eighteenth century, the area contains others to which no one style may be attributed. Such are Combe and Witley.

A Cistercian monastery was found at Combe in the reign of King Stephen, and the undercroft to the nineteenth-century

73 "THE SOFFITA OF THE GREAT STAIRCASE AT COMBE. PERFORMED BY MR. EDWARD GOUGE, PLAISTERER, 1678 ": with Captain Wynne's signature

east elevation does in fact consist of such Norman monastic work, carefully incorporated by Nesfield in his restoration; on this follow the late Gothic cloisters, the Jacobean fore-court and south-west building, the Palladian north and west elevations, and of course the Nesfield building; for a parallel to this last section it would be necessary to revive the first Memorial Theatre at Stratford. We know also from a letter of Elizabeth, wife of William, Earl Craven, that Lancelot Brown " laid out £10,000 " on the garden and estate at Combe. The house is thus a synopsis of English domestic building; it is perhaps most valuable for being an example

74 HONINGTON HALL, NEAR SHIPSTON

75 THE GARDEN FRONT, CROOME COURT

76 THE OCTAGON ROOM, HONINGTON

of the work of Captain Wynne, a mysterious and romantic figure whose hand appears also in an excellent brick house, dressed with stone, at Ramsbury in Wiltshire, and in two remarkable designs, both since destroyed, one for Buckingham House (on the site of the present Palace) and the other a great mansion at Hampstead Marshall in Berkshire, of which nothing remains but some formidable garden gate piers and a collection of drawings in the Bodleian library (73). This west front, dated 1684, is a very happy addition, and Buck's view shows the house as it was before Nesfield got at it. Nesfield, much like Habershon at Hadzor, graduated from scholarship to practice by way of a skilful dedication, and introduced, apart from the east elevation, a waterway, part moat and part Dutch canal, crossed by a medieval bridge copied from Chenonceaux. The great dining-room, and the apartments of Wynne's front, are full of curiosities—the brilliant white and gold, with curving pediments over doors and hearth, of the dining-room; the huge panels, massive cornice, and foliated woodwork of the brown parlour; the woodwork of the gilt parlour with its elaborate military devices and two rococo mirrors; and in Lady Craven's room the fireplace, inlaid with marble and without supporting figures, by Adam, and the late seventeenth-century plasterwork on the ceiling; there is also much work by Hondhorst, teacher to that Queen Elizabeth of Bohemia with whom the house has a permanent association, and tapestries after Teniers. Few houses can show such an olla podrida, in which avenues of armour (the gloomiest of bibelots) alternate with such marvels as the cabinet, attributed to Sheraton, in which are inlaid representations of castles and houses in fashion at the time, or the extraordinary state bed now in the brocatelle room. Not less interesting, again, than the lifelong sentimental attachment of the first Earl Craven to Elizabeth, daughter of James I. and Queen of Bohemia, is the career of Elizabeth, daughter of the Earl of Berkeley and wife of the sixth Earl Craven. A girl of great intellectual precocity, she at once set about altering her estates, giving her attention mostly to Benham and little to Combe, in which only the Adam fireplace and some pieces by Chippendale call attention to her passing. Her husband being a man of particular parts, but uncommonly fond of the play, she herself wrote a piece, called *The Miniature Picture* and produced at Drury Lane in 1680, with the authoress in a box, "naïvely aware," wrote an observer, "of her beauty and gifts." This did not suffice to keep Craven faithful, and in a little while she left for the Continent, where she at first lived with, and later married, the Margrave of Anspach, a nephew of Frederick the Great. Returning at his death to London, she met with a coldish reception, but lived on into the 1830s, entertaining with enormous verve in Brandenburg House at Hammersmith.

A mile or so from Droitwich, standing in a great park in which an abundance of dead and dying trees recalls a landscape of Graham Sutherland, is Hanbury Hall (65), built in 1701 by Thomas Vernon, a great Whig, prominent for forty years in the Court of Chancery and later M.P. for Worcester. This was a discriminating family of patrons, for not only is Hanbury itself an enchanting design, but the interior is decorated by Thornhill and in the parish church stands the first of three monuments commissioned in this neighbourhood from Roubiliac; when it is considered that Roubiliac was chosen for this Bowater Vernon monument above Scheemakers, Cheere, and Rysbrach, and that examples of Thornhill's work, after the fire at Stoke Edith and the bombing of Guy's Hospital, are exceedingly rare, it will appear in what a debt we stand to this family. Hanbury is almost a severe design, picked out by the two columns which appear to support the pediment; it is less an original building than an exceedingly well-bred one, in which such normal features as plain fenestration and small dormers, the dressing of the corners with stone, and the regular cornice at the eaves, are presented as if one had never seen them before. There is also an orangery, and at the back of the house a detached long, narrow gallery, difficult to use, but a charming survival. Of the decorations it is difficult to speak, since to the slow depreciation of time has now been added the re-verberation of nearby artillery-fire (66). Thornhill, a pupil of Thomas Highmore and father-in-law of Hogarth, had been abroad, and studied from Poussin, Veronese, and Lebrun; he had assisted Laguerre and worked with Verrio; and if he was not a painter of individual genius he was an experienced decorator, able to point a myth with topical allusion, used to payment by the yard, and at his best in the beautiful slack rhythms of his flying figures. At Stoke Edith, across the border of Herefordshire, he had a happier subject, with more

vistas, more seated and flying, and fewer standing, figures ;
more women, also, and at Hanbury it is the female figures
which come off best ; one could have wished also for a
greater element of *trompe l'œil*, than which nothing more
quickly enlivens decorative painting of this kind. Nevertheless this is valuable work, and there is, in addition, a tiny
drawing by Thornhill of the house and garden which shows
a just appreciation of its beauties.

An admirer of landscape gardening said of one of its
masters : " Mahomet imagined an Elysium, but Kent created
many." This is a controversial subject, and there are many
who think, with Johnson, that such gardening is " the sport,
rather than the business, of human reason " ; or who would
copy Peacock's Dr. Marmaduke Milestone, who, when informed that the dominant advantage of landscape gardening
was that of surprise, asked : " Pray, sir, how do you distinguish
this attribute when walking round a second time ? " Yet
the elder Pitt, who is not usually thought a frivolous or an
ineffective figure, himself laid out a walk at Wickham, in
Kent, and is thought to have had a hand at Hagley ; and it
might be thought that life could not be more agreeably
passed than in a universe of one's own creation. Examination will nevertheless prove this to be false.

The northern corner of Worcestershire includes the two
contiguous estates of Hagley and Halesowen, and these were
laid out at, roughly, the same time by two men, differing
indeed in station and parts, but contemporaries, and each born
within a couple of miles of the other. The one, Shenstone,
was later to dedicate his work, *Judgment of Hercules*, to the
other, Lord Lyttelton, and support him at the elections of
1740. Both created remarkable visions, and neither can be
accounted happy or successful. In later life Shenstone even
began to question his neighbour's whole attitude to their
work :

> " Will Lyttelton the rural landskip range,
> Leave noisy fame, and not regret the change ?
> Pleas'd will he tread the garden's early scenes,
> And learn a moral from the rising greens ? "

Lyttelton certainly was not of a happy disposition and had
retired from no very successful public life ; called by Gray
" a gentle, elegiac person," he was not in place in the world
of Chesterfield, to whom his habit of abstraction during meals

K

was specially abhorrent. "Wrapped up like a Laputan in intense thought," he says, "and possibly sometimes in no thought at all, he does not know his most intimate acquaintance by sight, or answers them as if they were at cross purposes." When nineteen years old he attended the Congress of Soissons, but took no pleasure in hunting nor in the society either of Frenchmen or of Englishmen, preferring to read Latin in solitude. Poyntz, the English ambassador, remarked his "interruptions of health, proceeding from ill digestion itself brought on by too lively and absenting an imagination." Nor could he find pleasure nearer at home ; at Vauxhall he said, "I always suppose pleasure to be in the next box to mine." In the House, he spoke constantly, but not well, in opposition to Walpole ; and when his party was in power he became Chancellor of the Exchequer, despite an inaptitude for figures ; indemnified at the end of this term with a peerage, he settled to twenty years' work on his "Henry II.," only to hear Gibbon speak of this "voluminous work, in which sense and learning are not illuminated by a ray of genius." To read the proofs of this he employed a man, by profession a maker of combs, so unlettered that nineteen pages of errata were needed. He put Thomson's *Coriolanus* on the stage ; was lampooned by Cobbett ; wrote a dialogue after Fontenelle, and received from Voltaire those two letters which are among the glories of Hagley; a freethinker, he flirted with Methodism.

Shenstone had no ambition of public life, and had been from his early years a literary fetichist of the most advanced kind ; such a great reader was he that he wished always to take a new book to bed with him, and when the supply of these ran short, he could be pacified only on receiving as substitute a block of wood wrapped in a towel. These pretentions were encouraged by residence at Pembroke College, Oxford ; at this (the original "nest of singing birds" and the home later of Beddoes) he remained for ten years without taking a degree. On returning to Halesowen in 1745, he at once began, in Johnson's words, "to point his prospects, to diversify his surface, to entangle his walks, and to wind his waters." The result was more modest than Hagley, and was indeed no more than a very pretty grazing farm ; but Walpole held it "a perfect picture of Shenstone's mind : simple, elegant, and amiable." Relations between the two estates

77 IN ROBERT ADAM'S GALLERY, CROOME COURT

78 WARWICK CASTLE, FROM THE AVON

were not entirely harmonious ; the greater resources and more
exuberant invention of Hagley used sometimes to excite
resentment in Shenstone, and visitors to the lesser estate
were not encouraged to linger at that point from which the
view of the greater was particularly fine. And whereas Hagley
is a stunning house, at Halesowen both house and estate were
neglected for their master's obsession ; tenants defaulted,
and through the broken roofs of the house (a poor one in
the first place) rain used often to flood the floors. Shenstone
lived with his housekeeper, and it is said that his death followed
upon a cold caught when, having quarrelled with her, he spent
the night in a postchaise. He affected privacy in the hope
of being sought out, and on his rare excursions to Oxford
hoped always (and with engaging indifference) to be mistaken
by undergraduates for " Pope, or Mr. Dodsley." He dressed
plainly, and wore his own hair, and could not for this reason
pass through the lodge of All Souls without exciting ridicule ;
and on the return journey his habits were such that Dr.
Alexander Carlyle, having a pony that stopped at every inn
door, named it " Shenstone." Yet there was a real idealism in his gardening, and Mrs. Piozzi records that nothing
so angered him as to be asked if there were fishes in his
ornamental streams.

Little now remains of Halesowen, and it could even be
said that the monastic remains and the monument by Thomas
Banks in the parish church are more fascinating than this
forlorn remnant; but Hagley is as astonishing as ever (69, 70).
The interior of the house, thanks to the scrupulous and creative
restoration undertaken after the fire of fourteen years ago,
approaches, more closely perhaps than at any time since its
erection, to the intention of its designers. Excellently plain
from without, and approached by a high perron, the house
is an ideal specimen of anglicised Palladian ; this style was
chosen only after much disputation, and Lady Lyttelton in
particular fought hard to secure a house " in the Greek
style," forcing her husband in 1752 to write to Sanderson
Miller in this sense ; others advised a Gothic structure,
something to match the sham ruin erected on the estate and
crusted, in Walpole's phrase, " with the true rust of the
Barons' wars." Once inside, however, the convenience of
the plan employed is readily apparent, for Hagley even in
war-time is a companionable, never a forbidding, house.

The plasterwork, which in the hall and salon astonishes by
its brilliance, wit, and invention, is by Vessali, an Italian
virtuoso who collaborated with Artari at Sutton Scarsdale
and at Ditchley with Serena (70). He is equally at home in
allegorical subjects (as in his " Sacrifice to Diana ") and in
the decorative motifs of the salon, in which venery, drama,
music, warfare, and husbandry are successively extolled. The
whole of the house was furnished by Chippendale's, and from
this commission the mirrors, brackets, picture-frames, and
one exceedingly fine chest have all survived the fire ; in the
long gallery the girandoles especially abound in fantasy, and
these have come safely out of the hazard imposed at one
time by the winter-practising of this great cricketing family.
This gallery, with its great columns of gold and white, picked
out in green, has an intimate brilliance unequalled by any
house in the area ; the library, surveyed by Scheemaker's
busts of Shakespeare, Milton, Spenser and Dryden, and
Richardson's portrait of Pope; and the tapestry-room, in which
for the original Gobelins has been substituted work from the
Soho shop of Joshua Morris and portraits by Allan Ramsay
of Lyttelton's five closest associates, pull one's attention back
and forward across the hall. The pictures at Hagley are not
restricted to the Lelys and Van Dycks, though these each
suffice to fill entire apartments, but include portraits also by
Wilson (this a great rarity), by Reynolds (one in the style of
Van Dyck and one belonging originally to Mr. Thrale's
famous set at Streatham), and by Pompeo Battoni, an enchanting neglected eighteenth-century portrait painter. Bassano
and Cornelis de Lyon ably contest for those last flickers of
æsthetic energy which may have survived this feast. Here,
in this very exceptional house, and not less than at Ferney,
one might sense the presence of Voltaire (who somewhere
quotes verses of Lyttleton as characterising the English
race) ; or of Frederick the Great, who presented one of the
books in the library ; or of that Frederick, Prince of Wales,
who stands in Roman dress upon a lofty column surveying
the house. A whole book could very pleasantly be written
while thinking of Hagley.

Ragley, Honington, and Croome come to mind when
leaving Hagley. The decoration, on motifs from Homer, at
both Honington and Ragley, is thought to be by Charles
Stanley, an Anglo-Danish artist who lived in England only

between 1726–46; these Trojan scenes apart, Honington, one of the most finicky, *manièré* houses in England, offers unending pleasure to amateurs of this period (74, 76). Not only is the plaster remarkable, but there are some of those leather panels, painted with Chinese scenes, which were fashionable in Holland from the middle seventeenth century and imported to England by connoisseurs. The ornamenta-

[*Drawn by Sydney R. Jones*

79 STUDLEY MANOR-HOUSE, WARWICKSHIRE

tion of even the smallest rooms at Honington is phenomenally rich, and in the great octagonal room (76), dominated by the " Venus Rising from the Sea " of Luca Giordano, even the glazing bars of the windows are moulded to set off the care lavished on the panel moulds of the shutters. The exterior, with its hipped roof, cornice, and slightly projecting wings (74), is curious for the series of Roman busts, on the lines of those made by Giovanni di Majano for Hampton Court, which surmount the ground-floor windows ; these are interesting as showing the close conjunction of Italy with ancient Rome in the mind of this time; one might compare the journal of Goethe's father, who valued things seen on his Italian tour in proportion as they led him to Imperial inscriptions.

Ragley, by the Arrow, and enclosed in a park of unusual magnificence, is a fine bold mansion, designed by Ripley and with an Ionic portico. Not all houses, however, were upon this scale; and other pursuits than the Turkish warfare commemorated by Vessali recur upon these humbler walls. At Kyre, for instance, near Tenbury, the growing of hops is the theme of the boudoir ceiling—and this although their cultivation was at this very time the subject of bitter controversy.

John Murray, in his Guides, had a charming custom which, if re-introduced, would greatly reduce the labour of topographical writers. For whereas normally he describes the more modest houses at length, it sometimes happens that, before a greater house, he is dumb; like Roger Fry before a last-period Cezanne, he is finished; and he simply inserts the opinion of a nobleman. Thus I find at random, " ' Ragley is superb—that is, the situation and dimensions of the house '—Lord Orford." I wish sometimes that I could get away as easily; I would even make do with a baronet; but at Croome, as at Hagley and Mere and Maxstoke, I would reject the considered judgment even of a Duke. Croome is a composite house, and it is a specialist task to disentangle the parts played in it by Sanderson Miller, Lancelot Brown— and also, on some views, of Adam. The south-west front, apart from its smaller perron, is like a more worked-up Hagley; and the garden front, by Miller, is of the restrained classic style copied later at Strensham Court (75). The stables, conservatory, entrance gates (these among the best monumental efforts of Robert Adam), rotunda, and panorama tower are all uncommonly pretty, and redemption of the sodden morass which is now an undulant, heavily timbered and beautifully varied estate, must rank among his greatest feats. Within is much work by Adam; but an attempt to split his commission with Chippendale caused him, in a fit of pique, to leave part of the long gallery unfinished, so that, although two sizeable marble girls uphold the fire-place, and others are placed in niches to either side, the reliefs are represented simply by sketches in oil (77). The house

81 COMPTON VERNEY, FROM THE LAKE

80 STONELEIGH ABBEY

WARWICKSHIRE PALLADIANISM

had formerly a set of astonishing Boucher tapestries, comparable to those at Newby, but these have since appeared in the rue de la Boëtie. The library is lined with bookcases of powerful mahogany, and contains many contemporary works on architecture ; a room upstairs is papered with a Chinese wallpaper, differing from that at Westwood in that vistas, rather than vegetation, are its subject, and much ingenuity appears in its coherent, yet never repetitive, scheme. The house in general is rather a collection of features than a single creation ; Adam, for example, worked at it on and off for thirty years ; and it suffers, perhaps, from being, in modern terms, an unwieldy house, unable to acquire the bloom of continuous living which distinguishes many smaller houses in the area. The personal history of the Coventry family is for the most part one of public service and encouragement of hunting ; thus the Croome hounds have recently been maintained largely by their efforts, and earlier members of the family have been (1425) Lord Mayor of London, (1606) Chief Justice of the Common Pleas, and, in the middle seventeenth century, Sir William Coventry was Secretary to the Admiralty and a great figure in the Diary of Pepys. Little, either in the family history or in his own character, prepares us, in fact, for the romantic story of the sixth Earl, creator of Croome. Chesterfield calls him " a grave young lord," and even when married to his intoxicating wife he would refuse an invitation to the fête of St. Cloud in order to attend a music-meeting at Worcester. The incalculable element in his story is, in short, the young person, " scarce a gentlewoman, but by her mother," Miss Maria Gunning, whose portrait by Reynolds is still at Croome. She and her sister were of impoverished origin, and when in Dublin were driven into the street by bailiffs ; their début in society was made possible only when Sheridan, then manager of a theatre in Dublin, lent them costumes from his professional stock. The phenomenal charm and irresistible persons of these two young women have been many times described ; not so the curious diversity between their husbands. For Coventry would never have been brought to the mark, for all his devotion, if it were not for the attention paid to the younger of the pair by the Duke of Hamilton—a young man, " hot, debauched, extravagant, and equally damaged in fortune and in person." Hamilton made love to the younger while losing at faro ; Coventry, moving the Address in the Lords, had the elder at his side. He made no move, and wagers were freely laid against his making one ; " most people," said Chesterfield, " expect a settlement, I a marriage." He was right ; for one morning at a quarter to one, Hamilton married the younger, in Mayfair chapel, and with a ring from the bed-curtains as pledge, and Coventry soon after left for the Continent with his bride. It was not a happy match, for he was jealous and prudish, and in 1760 his wife, who for several years had had the use, when walking in the Park, of a sergeant and twelve privates of the Guard for her personal protection, died of white-lead poisoning. A portrait of her sister and the Duke of Hamilton by Reynolds was formerly at Hadzor.

The banks of the Avon throughout its length invite the building of houses. Warwick Castle (78), Charlecote (17), and Guy's Cliffe, different in all else, unite in this ; and Stoneleigh (80, 82), most near of all these to its source, has in front of it a broad lake-like stretch of water. This, like Combe, was once a Cistercian abbey, one of those five hundred-odd communities which sprang up within half a century around Abbot Robert of Citeaux. Though a small abbey, one of the first to be dispossessed in 1536, it was used as a bank by the Despensers, allies of Edward II. against the barons, and broken into by his enemies, some £60,000 in our money being lost to the King. The house now visible is for the most part of 1720, when Lord Leigh erected an immense west building with towering Ionic pilasters, deep cornice, and balustrade (80). The monastic remains were heavily restored in Jacobean times, and it is the formal Victorian gardens (including oaks planted by the Queen and her consort) and the sumptuous interior which now retard the visitor ; for the unidentified plaster decorations, the great oak staircase, and the quasi-royal magnificence of the salon combine to impress, and perhaps to exhaust, the most ambitious eye (82). Smith of Warwick, who built this west building of Stoneleigh, Sanderson Miller, and Thomas White, pupil of Wren and civic architect of Worcester, are three first-rate native architects of this area. The iron gates (reputedly by a pupil of Tijou) and the curious enveloping walks and bowers of ivy, planted three years after Waterloo, are also features of Stoneleigh.

It is difficult, however much one may admire the men of

Soho, to give examples of their houses, for most of these—
most indeed of the red-brick eighteenth-century Birmingham
—no longer survive. Bombing and industrial necessity are
completing a process which, a few years ago, had still left
Temple Row, for instance, Cannon Street and Moor Street,
and the corner of Newhall Street and Edmund Street as
fragments of this charming town. John Baskerville, however,
was born in 1706 at Sion Hill, Wolverley, near Kidderminster,
and various traces of him may still be found. Baskerville
was not simply a person to whom all writers, printers, and
publishers are indebted, but at once a propagandist, seeking
to encourage appreciation of the classics and of the best
contemporary authors, by the éclat and amenity of his editions,
and also a forerunner of such craftsmen as Morris and Eric
Gill; for the peculiar charm of his books proceeded from
his making the inks himself and preparing a special kind of
paper. There was much bidding for his type at his death,
and in the end it was secured by Beaumarchais for a fantastic
project comprising the editing, printing, and publication by
a learned society (consisting entirely in the person of Beaumarchais) of a definitive edition of Voltaire; many volumes
of this appeared, often simultaneously, from several European
capitals, but I do not know if the type was used to its original
effect.

The birthplace of Burne-Jones is known, and that of
Elgar at Broadhurst, near Worcester; and that Alfred
Baldwin who died worth a quarter of a million pounds can
probably be traced to a harmless brick-faced eighteenth-century
house. In Birmingham itself, however, even the quality of
the material works against survival; for the local clay is
unsuitable for cut brickwork, and any ornament is of stone;
thus the houses are in general plain outside, though often
surprisingly elegant within, and can make no show of being
indispensable. In other towns, no house with personal
associations is quite as pretty as Landor's at Warwick; and
for a great house, the last utterance of the eighteenth century
in this area, we must go to the country, to Compton Verney (81)
Even here there is already a compromise, for the state rooms
were done over, and the swag frieze under the portico and
the entrance to the hall designed by John Gibson, a pupil
of Charles Barry, in 1855. Yet it also looks back, this urbane
and water-rounded house, for the stable block is thought to

L

be by Leoni, the Italian architect who prepared the works of Palladio for English publication.

Compton Verney is essentially a social house, used to being on a main road and receiving travellers; it was never, like Compton Wynyates, a hidden retreat, reached by few tracks and conspicuous only as one breasted the great bowl and looked into the hollow. It is partly by Adam, partly by Vanbrugh, a collaboration less curious than is often supposed, for Adam admired Vanbrugh; " in point of movement, novelty, and ingenuity," he said, " he is not exceeded by anything in modern times." Vertue dates the Vanbrugh section at 1714, and the south-west front, with its bold outline and arched windows, corresponds to other work of this artist (81); the Doric pilasters and broken centre of the entablature also point to his hand, while his sash-barring was lost in the plate-glass frenzy of the middle nineteenth century. The part of Adam in the house is thought to have been in celebration of the marriage of John Peyto, fourteenth Baron Willoughby de Broke, to Lady Louisa North, sister of the Prime Minister, Lord North, in 1761, and certainly his additions are such as a marriage might occasion; that is to say that he prolonged the north and south façades, making the original end pavilion of Vanbrugh the middle of the south front, added a portico on the east front, and knocked out a cross wall to transform hall and dining-room into the present great hall, with two apsidal ends and an entrance through the middle. He built also an orangery and the bridge of three segment arches; these fall well in with the occasional architecture in which this area is rich; they compare, for instance, with the Doric temple of Athenian Stuart at Hagley, and the Temple Seat by James Wyatt at Croome. Mention of Wyatt, however, brings us properly over the border and into the century of Toddington, Ashridge, and Witley.

Witley is an estate of honourable lineage; it is, in fact, a dynastic structure, the product of several centuries of successful commerce, for though in origin an Elizabethan house, it was first enlarged, and the demesne exploited, by the grandson of Thomas Foley, the proprietor of an ironworks which, during the Civil Wars, happened to come by considerable profits. This grandson became Lord Foley in 1711, and built in 1725 a mansion in the Italian style, now hardly to be noticed in the ironmonger's gala let loose a hundred years later by

83 THE WATER-GARDENS AT WESTBURY COURT ON SEVERN, from Kip's engraving of *c.* 1727

a new owner, Lord Ward of Himley; here, as at Combe, W. A. Nesfield was employed; but having here no medieval remnants on which to build, he gave himself full rein. Discounting the house (in which, however, Queen Adelaide, widow of William IV., resided in luxury for four years) we may consider the garden and waterworks, on which Nesfield lavished his art; the fountain of Perseus and Andromeda (a subject of the highest convenience in this form of art) is not merely in itself a formidable mass of metal, but employs in its service an apparatus totalling 1400 yards in length and reaching at times a height of 160 feet; a certain rude magnificence must be conceded to this project. At Westbury-on-Severn one may in contrast admire the lilies and flanking pavilions of a Dutch garden, one of the first to be built in England, and one of the most perfect water-gardens existing (83, 141).

Sacheverell Sitwell considers the planting of such long avenues as that of Badminton as the mark of settled religious belief; and a similar confidence in the future may be presumed in amateurs of topiary. Wren may not have known that his topiary fort, erected at Hampton Court, would have a chance of surviving many of his city churches; but there is no doubt about the endurance of the work at Rous Lench Court, where the invention of the Chafy family and the fortunate inclination of the estate have allowed of an enormous area of this simple and rudely humorous ornament.

It is difficult to give an account of nineteenth-century building, in that a catalogue of horrors would unfairly ignore the excellent Regency and William IV. done everywhere, in towns and villages and small estates, by tradesmen-architects; much of the aspiration of later architects was civic or devotional, so that, churches apart, school buildings— those of Rugby and Malvern, for example—have to be taken in. Work of this period has been little collated, and it is convenient to begin with Repton, who built Dumbleton Hall, in Gloucestershire, and laid out its park about 1830. Rickman, one of the pioneer apologists for his time, can be seen at Down House, a manor in the Grecian style at Staunton. Of Hadzor House and village we have already some idea; but my own preference is for Spetchley Park, near Worcester, for this mansion of 1810, in the German style yet with

84   TODDINGTON MANOR, GLOUCESTERSHIRE

85 DEERHURST CHURCH: Saxon and Gothic

86 GLOUCESTER CATHEDRAL FROM THE AIR

an Ionic portico, has a mile-long avenue of elms before it ; near to this also is the 1848 Italian manor of Bricklehampton Hall. It is, however, to Lord Sudeley, an amateur of building, that we must concede the palm, and if there is any fault to be found with our illustration of Toddington (84) it is that the interior, a fascinating essay in Barry's Houses of Parliament manner, may naturally not be seen from it.

We began with the first units of social building—the manor and the castle and the barn. We shall end with an attempt to recapture the old consistency of this essential group ; for at Huntley in Gloucestershire, Teulon has built a manor (in the French Château style), a vicarage and school, and rebuilt the church ; except for the church tower this nucleus is, in fact, entirely of 1860, and may serve to epitomise the prodigious energy of these great sedulous creatures who never entered a railway carriage without leaving it littered with new designs (Scott indeed had a special coach designed to allow him complete liberty of inspiration). Later building has a certain horrid fascination, but I cannot compete with that casuistry of taste which makes a little shrine of Malvern Gothic and the homes of the robber dynasties of Edgbaston. If I had to choose, I would have the leafy Long-Island outskirt of Coventry ; for as one runs through this from Kenilworth, it seems to promise a sight, not of the burnt acres of Coventry City Centre, but of the long-rolling North Atlantic beaches.

86A OLD HAGLEY HALL, FROM A DRAWING
OF 1758

V

CHURCHES IN THE SHAKESPEARE COUNTRY

THOSE ignorant of ecclesiology might put it among gentle pastimes, along perhaps with brass-rubbing or the pursuit of inscriptions. They might even expect that those whose hobby is in visiting the houses of God would be meek and of a yielding disposition. Nothing of the kind; ecclesiology was founded by energetic and contentious young men, and has been kept alive by others of similar stamp; Rickman and the Pugins were always brawling; and even to-day I believe that a timid man is safer in the society of bruisers than in that of people newly won over to geometrical tracery. Cathedrals, however, are great levellers; their great size and antiquity make of them a repository in which everyone must find some occasion for joy. Not here are the single combats excited by those smaller churches where a tympanum, a group of five lancets at the east end, a Jacobean table, or a monument by John Bushnell will variously inflame the passion of specialists; in a cathedral each may find his level, and, raising at random the opera-glasses essential to the enthusiast, sweep successively the full height of the vaulted nave and apse, the hundred and thirty sculptured bosses and the great window to the west, lingering finally (in time of service, and if rumour be not unjust) upon the tenanted quire. Our journey will be the more peaceful in that the Shakespeare country, having been so much under monastic rule and ownership, is distinguished rather by its greater than by its lesser churches.

Let us nevertheless consider, first, two survivors of an age previous to that in which the monasteries were found to own well over half of Worcestershire. At Deerhurst, reached by foot and across orchard country from Tewkesbury, standing among the Severn meadows, is a Saxon church (85). It is a curious exception to the rule that the Danish invasions were uniformly destructive, for both here and at Forthampton and Bishop's Cleeve are details of Scandinavian origin in the otherwise rude and wide-jointed ragwork of the tower, some of whose angles have herringbone work, others being finished long and short. Originally a long narrow cruciform building with apsidal quire and north and south quire chapels, it was extended to include north and south aisles, and on the Early English arcades of these there are some elegant sculptured capitals ; the font is of the tenth century and very pretty (115B). Though known as a Saxon church, Deerhurst has picked up many interesting adornments since ; the chancel is one of those few still to show

87 BRASS AT DEERHURST TO JUDGE SIR JOHN CASSY, ALICE HIS WIFE, AND HER DOG TERRI, 1400

the Puritan arrangement of seating for communicants; and the brass (1401) of Sir John Cassy and his wife is a beauty and includes one of the three named pets in English work of this kind (87). Here and in the nearby Cotswolds is a little nest of Saxon work such as has wholly gone from Warwickshire, that cockpit of invasions; at Wooton Wawen, however, the base of the tower, its first two stages, and four doorways are known to be Saxon work. At Deerhurst there is also a chapel curiously close to the church and abutting on to a timbered farmhouse; it is of blue lias, with wide mortar joints, and hardly touched since its erection as chantry chapel in 1056; it is in a beautiful position, is reached by a varied and beautiful walk, and contains, among other bric-à-brac, a curious head, with the

88 CARVING ON THE TYMPANUM OF THE RUINED
NETHERTON CHAPEL, UNDER BREDON HILL

oval eyes and wilful mouth of the young Beethoven, for which nobody, at the time of my visit, could satisfactorily account. Another side of Norman work is seen at Netherton chapel, near Elmley Castle. This is in the kind of disrepair which must have afflicted Anglican churches in the time of the Georges; as early as the fourteenth century it is recorded as disused; in 1738 it was turned into a barn; and in this state it was sketched by Prattinton the antiquary in 1812. It might, in fact, seem perverse to draw attention to it, if it were not for the tympanum above the south door (88). This narrative of the winged saw-fish is one of those early Christian phenomena in which the most bold and elaborate concepts are enunciated with perfect clarity and assurance to an audience as yet uncorrupted by verbal convention; in this case the fish, a poor flyer, is a symbol of " this world, which flies

89   TEWKESBURY ABBEY

90 BESFORD CHURCH, NEAR PERSHORE

91 IN THE AMBULATORY, TEWKESBURY

vigorously for a little way and is then drawn beneath the waters to hell as soon as the impetus of greed, pride, drunkenness, and luxury is spent." Let us at once, and before one or a combination of these faults allows us also to be submerged, proceed to examine a major monument of this region.

There are moods and places and times of the day and year in which Tewkesbury Abbey (89, 91, 93) is, of all English sights, the most wholly satisfying ; to these has recently been added its tantalising evocation of ton upon ton of butter piled up into the clean valley air. This, in contrast to much of the best domestic work we shall see, is pre-eminently serious building, thought out in terms of this particular kind of stone and executed with wonderful address and independence of detail. Nothing could better celebrate the confluence of Severn with Avon than this great Norman tower and the sixfold recession of the arch at the west end ; this exterior, being dependent on mass and proportion rather than on surface and ornament, is difficult to photograph, and comes out best in a drawing of Turner ; but the whole church is an excellent introduction to the area, since it summarises the wealth of fine Norman work to be expected in a monastic region, foreshadows in its Decorated quire vaulting the full flowering of this style in the south aisle of Gloucester Cathedral, and provides in its ambulatory a miniature guide to both that and the succeeding indigenous Perpendicular, dawning at Gloucester, whose freedom from early Renaissance influence is one of the miracles of our architecture. The Norman porch and the fourteen great cylinders of the nave leave one unready for that upward glance which reveals complex lierne-vaulting sprung on its corbels from the very capitals of the pillars ; the growth and sumptuous ornament of this interior is indeed a story of consistent prosperity and participation in affairs— whereas that of Gloucester, for instance, is halting and irregular. The many carved bosses of the nave-vaulting repay painful scrutiny ; one series especially, that of an angelic orchestra, is, like the parallel at Gloucester of the greatest technical interest. The same mingling of Norman and Decorated work occurs in the quire, and in the bays to either side of this are the three great fourteenth- and early fifteenth-century chantries ; these typify an epoch for which nothing was finer than building, nothing a more ample employment for man. As Lethaby said, " the folk had fallen in love with building, and loved that their goldsmith's work, and ivories, their seals, and even the pierced patterns of their shoes should be like little buildings, little tabernacles, little 'Paul's windows.' "

One of the many little sculptured groups in Worcester Cathedral shows a monk holding in his hand a tiny model of a cathedral; such, in effect, are these chantries (91); even more elaborate in their towering canopies are the two early fourteenth-century tombs of Hugh Despencer and Guy de Brien. The effigy in none of these is of much importance; the whole trend of provincial work was that consummated by the Purbeck marblers who from 1460–1560 turned out recessed and canopied chantries, without effigies, in imitation of these noble originals. The Despencer Chapel is unique for its time in that the effigy kneels; this posture was refused to Henry VII. by Torregiano even many years later. The Wakeman cenotaph is a fine case of overheated flamboyant Decorated, and its pendanted ogee and congested crocketing fall in very well with the ghoulish treatment of the cadaver (93). It is interesting also to compare the small Clarke monument of Flaxman with his shipwreck extravaganza in Gloucester Cathedral. The marvel of Tewkesbury, however, is its review of the monastic achievement, and no one could visit it without fleeting conversion to this way of life. Yet the parish church is necessarily a mixed affair, and no matter with what particular interest one may enter, one is sure to leave with the emphasis displaced; suppose, for instance, that a pilgrim, inflamed by the Norman wonders of Tewkesbury, wishes to see Norman work in another part of the area—at Beaudesert or Berkswell. At Beaudesert, a few hundred yards from Henley-in-Arden, no trouble arises; the east window is a specimen of elaborate but rather dim Norman ornament, with multi-chevroned arch, diaper and diamond ornament, and cushion-capped jamb-shafts. Of the chancel arch, even more private language can be used, for in addition to the triple rows of chevron, pellet, and zigzag ornament, there are the chamfered abaci which foreshadow the piers of Early English arcading. Only the embattled fifteenth-century tower distracts from these early fragments; but at Berkswell one is met at first sight, not by the hardly altered Norman chancel, nor, in the nature of things, by the octagonal Saxon crypt, but by a seventeenth-century addition—the half-timbered upper storey to the south

porch. Timbered churches do not, of course, take kindly to
the neglect of centuries, and it is not much more than fifty
years since a proposal to demolish Besford church, near
Pershore, and an entirely half-timbered structure of the
fourteenth century, was only narrowly rejected. Besford is
timbered inside as well as out, and the sixteenth-century
panelling and Laudian altar rails would be remarkable even
without the great prize of this church—its rood loft crossing
intact fron north to south, with roses in each of the quatre-
foils which ornament its panels (90); the homage done here
to the rose recalls the tulip-mania that followed the Restoration, and of the two this is the more enduring. Also at
Besford are a monument and painted triptych to Edmund
Harewell, who died in 1576 at the age of fifteen; this was
an indifferent transitional period for provincial monuments,
and I cannot feel that either of these is very good; the triptych
especially is not a patch on that of a hundred years later at
Alcester. But Besford, seen in conjunction with the nearby
manor and L-shaped barn, is a fine example of wooden
vernacular.

A church with Norman or pre-Conquest features will
naturally be overlaid with later work; but in effect there is
no style which will not give rise to a similar diversion of
interest. Consider, for instance, the remarkable church at
Lapworth in Warwickshire (95); this has three main uncommon
features—a detached tower of c. 1400 to the north-east, connected to the fabric by a modern vestibule; a tall and brilliant
late Perpendicular clerestory; and at the west end a two-
storeyed portico. This last we have already seen at Berkswell,
but the tower with its singular spire, and the great height
of the clerestory with its vigorous and dynamic ornamenta-
tion, are representative both of the area and of the time before
the Reformation when the church even of a small parish
could be a rich and powerful statement. The detached tower
is found also in the Herefordshire part of our area, at Bosbury
and Ledbury; the spire of Lapworth was rebuilt in the 1880s,
but in its extreme delicacy it resembles the two great eighteenth-
century spires executed at Ledbury and at St. Andrew's,
Worcester, by Nathaniel Wilkinson, stone-cutter to the
Cathedral of Worcester. These spires were an object of wonder
and pride to several generations, and once, at St. Nicholas' in
the 1790s, when a gale had dislodged some of its highest

stones, a barber ascended the scaffolding of the spire and shaved the workmen at its apex.

The clerestory of Lapworth is incidental to its many other fine features ; but the clerestory of Southam, some nine miles to the other side of Warwick, is its only remaining feature, for savage restoration has killed all but this great sixteen-lighted, floorless gallery. No church with such a clerestory can be wholly spoilt,[1] and one without any may find great inconvenience in its absence ; that of Pebworth, for example, on the Stratford-Honeybourne road, has had little dormer windows inserted in the roof to augment the light from the Perpendicular fenestration below. Pebworth is interesting also as having that rare thing—a piscina with really pretty rosette motifs ; piscinæ, though among the gloomiest elements in ecclesiology, are often thought to enchant the visitor by their very presence.

Lapworth, with its detached tower, has enticed us to the great churches of Bosbury and Ledbury ; but it may also lead us, by mistaken analogy, to St. Mary's, Warwick. Anyone who had left Lapworth with eyes ringing with the energy of Perpendicular work might well be taken with the dashing Gothic pinnacles and crocketing on the aisles of this church, even to the extent of mistaking it for genuine ; too little is made of Sir William Wilson and his church, and this, the first essay in Gothic reconstruction, is incomparably the best in the area, and could be rivalled only by such work as that of Jearred at Christ Church, Cheltenham ; this latter, however, for all its audacity, is fluky and uneven, whereas Wilson never loses the style associated with that Queen Anne who gave a thousand pounds towards this work. Warwick and the valley of the Arrow have several cases of this excellent eighteenth-century Gothic ; at Arrow itself the tower is said sometimes to be by Horace Walpole, and at Alcester the church inside and out is a model of what an unpretending market-town should be glad to have. Yet amateurs of this style appear, from the evidence of convention, to be a set of immoral boobies. Anyone not deterred by this will find the greatest pleasure in the work of Sanderson Miller at Kineton. Kineton was rebuilt in 1775 by Miller, an architect whose domestic work we have seen at Croome and

[1] Other examples of this fine Warwickshire clerestory-work occur at Fillongley and Wooton Wawen.

may find also at Radway, where Fielding, a great lover of this area, wrote much of *Tom Jones*. Only the tower of Kineton is original, but this wonderful piece of early fourteenth-century building is a worthy father of Warwickshire towers.

Any pretext, false or not, is welcome that takes us to St. Mary's. Wilson has made up a tower that sums up the

92   THE CHAPEL, TEMPLE BALSALL, before alteration

whole trend of Warwickshire towers and is yet a little more tricked-out than any, a little more urban. These towers of Warwickshire are very different from the battery of crouching and gargoyled projections which lie about Bredon; the train has no sooner crossed the border from Oxfordshire, at Cropredy, than the first of them (a poor one, admittedly) comes into view. Of three storeys or so, sometimes irregular in configuration, with battlement and slender belfry window, they have often two and sometimes three string-courses; the greatest of them, at Brailes, has a wonderful five-light

M

Perpendicular window, but mostly they are like those at Welford or Henley or Long Itchington, plain and hard-wearing ; at Snitterfield the tower, of the fifteenth century, is more squat ; at Wooton Wawen the two lower stages are Anglo-Saxon, and at Ufton the angles have each an ascending buttress with string-course carried round. But this is a suspicious preoccupation, and meanwhile our pilgrim has interrupted his study of St. Mary's to go posting off to a source of authentic medieval work—to Temple Balsall (92). Temple Balsall lies in pretty country and is reached by roads across which the shallow Blythe flows indifferently. Only its age, to an unfriendly eye, distinguishes it from Balliol chapel ; and only a specialist could prefer this relique of the Knights Templar and the Knights Hospitaller to the more genial work of other medieval orders ; it is late thirteenth-century work and has the feeling, common in this period, of a certain technical advance upon Norman building unaccompanied by any corresponding advantage of expression. The prize here, however (if we are unmoved by the piscina and aumbry which, it is said, "will be specially admired "), is the Geometrical tracery ; there are six little wheels at the sides, and at the west end a larger wheel with twelve spokes to it.

Church-visiting is a picaresque employment, and the visitor easily diverted ; thus, on the way to Ledbury, a wise traveller will cross into Herefordshire well north of Bromyard, taking in the lovely Teme country (122, 124–5) and leaving the road across the Malverns for the return journey. In this way he will take in the cluster of churches north of Bosbury, and in Worcestershire, Stanford and Shelsley Walsh.

Geology is rarely so directly attached to everyday life as in the church of Shelsley, for this is built mostly of travertine, or calcareous tufa, of which an enormous mass exists at Southstone Rock, a little way beyond the church ; this, moreover, has several antiquarian features—a remarkable collection, nearly equalling that at Malvern, of encaustic tiles, a twelfth-century font in the shape of an hour-glass, and a rood screen of the late fifteenth century which is as good as any in the county, the two rows of vine-leaf enrichment on the rood beam being particularly happy ; the fifteenth century, rather than the sixteenth, is indeed in many ways the age of dandyism in church appointments ; the Stafford monument of 1450, for instance, at Bromsgrove, is a display of quite exceptional

4 THE ABBEY BELL TOWER AND ST. LAWRENCE'S
CHURCH, EVESHAM

93 THE WAKEMAN CENOTAPH, TEWKESBURY

95 LAPWORTH CHURCH, WARWICKSHIRE

over-dressing, both in the armour, the baudric, bascinet, and surrounding orle of the male, and in the grotesque, jewelled and mitre-steep hair of the female. A little north of Shelsley, however, is Stanford, of which it would be provocative, at this stage, to say more than that it was built in 1768 ; inside, however, is the Winnington monument, the last of Roubiliac's three Worcestershire commissions, and erected to Thomas Winnington, who died of the attentions of a quack doctor called Thompson, whose powers Fielding rashly praised in some episodes (later suppressed) of *Amelia*. Winnington was Paymaster to H.M.'s Forces, a position of considerable amenity.

Pushing for the moment straight down to Ledbury, we are instantly aware of a church of a magnificence the more curious in that no substantial institution is known to have supported it. At close range its great irregularity of style detracts a little from the first impression ; nevertheless this, in wet weather particularly, is tremendous, for the churchyard, an uncommonly large one, is so set in relation to the church, that from each of its entrances the effect, enhanced by dripping foliage, is hauntingly fine. In point of fact the west end has a Norman door, three tall Early English arches, and Decorated windows ; the chancel arcade is Norman, the nave Perpendicular, with the north aisle earlier and more stiff than the south ; yet none of this affects the enduring romantic appeal of Ledbury. It is never very light in this church, and serious scrutiny of its many fine monuments is further hampered by their being all either high up on the walls, or else enclosed in twilit cages in which the student, crouched like a baboon behind the bars, is often surprised by less thoughtful visitors. For glass, however, these are excellent conditions, and the north chapel in particular, a large and sumptuous Decorated appanage, is worth visiting at dusk ; fragments of ancient glass have as companions at Ledbury, not the usual costly memorials of Crimea or the Spanish battalion, but a copy of one of Reynolds' windows at New College, and work also of Burne-Jones, in which the " almost suave nostalgia " of this artist strikes what one might have thought impossible— a newly contrasting note of distinction. This honour must be denied to the infantilist altar-tomb by Thorneycroft ; but Westmacott, a girlish, rather lascivious artist of whose individuality more might be made, comes off very nicely here and at Preston-on-Stour and Kenilworth ; at Worcester his military subject is not quite so happy. Flaxman, who has two examples, does very well ; but the Biddulph monument of 1718, reached by a kind of Mappin Terrace and usually in complete darkness, proves all these artists to have been not quite at their best.

Bosbury resembles Ledbury only in having a detached tower, and even here there is soon a point of divergence, for whereas Ledbury stands beneath the seventy yards of Wilkinson's spire, the tower of Bosbury is short and tough, having nothing in common with the " intelligent eyes " detected by George Eliot in the typical towers of Warwickshire, or with the neighbouring spires, panelled sides, niched figures, and blind-windowed belfries of Bromsgrove and King's Norton. It is of the thirteenth century, square and impenetrable, lit only by the same narrow lancets which (except to the east) light the church ; the pointed arches of the Transitioual arcade are consistent with this forbidding scheme, and it is indeed a curious place in which to find the work of a most charming indigenous decorative artist ; yet John Guldo of Hereford is nowhere represented in the area, but here.[1] Guldo gets into every text-book as the first sculptor to leave a signature embedded in his work ; but the two Harford monuments of 1573 and 1578 establish him by other criteria as someone very much out of the way. He had been to London, and is thought to have been employed by Henry VIII.; he would have seen the work of Italians, and it is to these that the rumours of Agostino and Pisanello in his work can be traced ; or the single heavy leaves, unlike anything in the vernacular, on the pediment of the earlier (97), and the single sprays and egg-and-tongue moulding on the later, some of these being held in the teeth of monsters. These are not always happy innovations ; there is the broken fluting of the pillars in the earlier, and the use of the sarcophagus which, though irreproachably Pisan, does not assist the design, and the figures in each case are awkward. All the same the moulding and placing of the flowered panels (themselves unknown in contemporary work) are admirably sensitive in the monument illustrated (97) ; in the other the ornament, though pretty enough in itself, has something of the value-for-money congestion of Burton work. Yet these two tombs bring something very uncommon—a breath of the hot, dry air disturbed in the passage through England of

[1] I have since been told of other, though inferior, examples at Astley and Madley. The exact spelling of his name may be Gildon.

Pietro di Torregiano, the first of the great paranoiac sculptors, breaker of Michaelangelo's nose, destined to die of melancholia in a prison at Seville.

Herefordshire had formerly a large indigenous school or sculptors in wood, but of these only one example, at Much Marcle, comes to mind ; and of the great romantic artist, Epiphanius Evesham, we have nothing, for although he was born at Wellington, and of good Herefordshire family, we should have to go as far as Hertfordingbury to find one or his astonishing tombs. Herefordshire is rich instead in an earlier decorative art, and at Castle Frome, six miles north of Ledbury, there is a Norman font in the idiom identified by Romilly Allen as descending from that of the Anglian school in Mercia (101); this font is typical of the elaborate visual idiom which it is almost impossible to reproduce for a people sophisticated by verbal convention. It stands upon three figures, part human and half beast, which are construed as sins expelled at baptism ; the bowl itself is encircled by a representation of the Baptism, each Person of the Trinity appearing in turn ; the audacity and entire success of this conception are worth going many miles to see. Rickman took the font at Chaddesley Corbett to be the type of late Norman work, but the dragons of this are no match for the birds, fish, and flying Spirit of Castle Frome, while the inter-laced ornament is no more than a school convention. At Cropthorne, one of the most wilfully pretty of English villages, there was found in the eighteenth century a cross-head free from all Celtic influence, fretted with a Greek device on its edge-face and with zoömorphs, key-patterns, and trilobed foliage upon its surface. Decoration of this kind found its own opportunities, and at Norton, not far from Cropthorne and quite as pretty, there is a lectern of Trans-itional work, with a seated bishop erect among boskage (101); [1] Holt has a font with heads of beasts, and Overbury one in which the church's founder appears, a model of the build-ing in his right hand ; and at Coleshill in Warwickshire there is a font of the latest and richest Norman invention. The Crucifixion upon the bowl of this font might be by some northern Castagno ; the alternate panels of foliage and manu-script-figures are, in comparison, no more than filling-in.

All these are the truest regional art, and it is almost com-forting to come upon less self-sufficing work. At Rous

[1] It came from Evesham Abbey, and has a first cousin, equally fine, at Crowle.

Lench, one of the most bizarre of English parish churches, there is a carved stone of two peacocks being offered grapes from a vine. This has obviously a Mediterranean ancestry, and is in fact a copy of some Lombardo-Byzantine original —the ambo at S. Salvatore in Brescia has been suggested; but its interest lies in the legend it illustrates. The bestiary, as a source of metaphor and parable, is often thought to be outmoded, but I do not know that there has been since the seventeenth century any new symbolism as good as that of these medieval series, and in this stone at Rous Lench this is combined with the orthodox Christian image of Christ as the True Vine. The peacock has for us something of that precedence among birds that the greyhound and spaniel were thought, by Sir Philip Sidney, to enjoy among dogs; but a bestiary of the thirteenth century supplies the key to the dolorous birds upon this stone, for the peacock is here compared " to the soul, which in the night of this world thinks that it has lost the grace of God and cries out in great distress with tears and prayers." The peacock motif reappears a few hundred yards from the church in a secular connection; for of the ten yew terraces of Rous Lench Court, some are scalloped, some are pierced and buttressed, some have gateways large enough to admit a carriage and four, and some are flanked by a representation in this same obliging medium of the Chafy crest—a peacock with tail spread. These ingenuities are best seen from a brick tower, some sixty feet high and built in imitation of an Italian campanile; this anomaly will prepare a thoughtful observer for the interior of the church. This is not wholly bizarre; it contains such continent features as a restored wheel window, a twelfth-century stone of Christ in glory, a Saxon aumbry with lavabo, and a fine pre-Reformation chalice; but this restored Norman and Early English building has been so bedizened by Florentine craftsmen imported for the purpose that it can resemble no other parish church in the country. It would be the worst kind of unthinking gentility to dismiss this church as an extravaganza; not only is it a valuable relic of the ultramontane Anglicanism of 1885, but it is even some sort of guide to the original appearance of our churches, for these were not always the uniform gruel-colour (varied only by patches of damp) which we have come to accept. This debility of colour is unthinkable in medieval decoration, and Rous Lench, the church, and

96   THE BEAUCHAMP CHAPEL, ST. MARY'S, WARWICK

98   THE COVENTRY MONUMENT, CROOME

97   ONE OF THE TWO MONUMENTS BY JOHN
GULDO, BOSBURY

the yellow peeling rectory, may be recommended as a new experience for the eye. This cannot, however, be said for the north chapel; this, a creation of 1885, is a kind of potting-shed in which are stored a number of bibelots, headed by the Rous monument of 1719, a scenic confection in which the mourning wife is consoled by the appearance, in full flight, of cherubs carrying a medallion of her husband. It is interest-ing, while remaining in this penthouse, to compare this with the same family's monument of 1611, in which the rigid descriptive convention of the time is lightened only by the Moor's head, a heraldic innovation recalling the Turks and Russians who had not long previously been entertained upon the frozen Thames.

Such treatment of monuments brings, by contrast, Elmley Castle to mind; the beauty of this village, the straight run of its main street to the very foot of Bredon, lead no longer to any castle, for even in Leland's time the last stones of its sur-viving tower were being carried off to repair the bridge at Pershore; instead, there is this church and its yard. The most desultory church-visitor in this area cannot fail to remark the excellence of many early nineteenth-century tombstones; but here there is a whole cluster of stones whose lettering and devices point to the existence of gifted local craftsmen. Two especially, of 1805 and 1828, have scenes from the life of Elijah, and others, less elaborate, have doves, or cherubs, or willows; all are worth looking at. The church, with em-battled nave and tower, is, in its structure, a typical restored Bredon building; but in one of its windows in the south aisle there is ancient glass in which, beneath a red rose, are quartered the arms of England and France—a collaboration which, though many times broken, has as many times brought beauty and wisdom and wealth to Europe, since the first friendship of Offa with Charlemagne. The Savage monu-ment of 1631 and 1674 is an aggregate of three lying and four small kneeling figures. Many of its passages are uncommonly good descriptive work, and the pearly, translucent alabaster was clearly a pleasure to work; opposite, and hiding the site of a Jesse window, is the Coventry monument of 1724, which was refused admission to Croome d'Abitot; the castellated wig, fine lace cravat, and monk's-hood shoes of this figure are typical of early Orange costume, and its happy placing in the church allows it to be seen, as it were, through a vista, so that the great architectural canopy and the semi-recumbent posture are seen to compose perfectly—a test rarely possible, in that few sculptors knew how their work would be placed, and many have been moved from one position to another.

About Bredon are many of these battlemented churches, with low towers of the fifteenth century, gargoyles (usually very poor ones), no clerestory, fragments of old glass inset in more recent designs, tombs of woollen merchants, and very often an engaging indifference to the punctilio of ecclesiology. At Little Comberton, for instance, the piscina is mounted on a drain-pipe, three ancient heads can be picked out in the glass, there are some eighteenth-century tiles, and a fine timber door of 1639. At Eckington there is an altar table of 1663, a red-headed angel of the fourteenth century in one pane of glass, an arcade with differing capitals, and a fine monument of 1616 to John Hanford, the builder of Woolas Hall. This full-bellied founder appears with his wife, five sons, and eight daughters ; enumeration upon this scale set new problems for the sculptor, who introduced the kneeling convention, and finding this insufficient, used to fill the sides, back, and even the arch-moulding (a kind of *strapontin* for younger sons) with children. In this case the cloak, flared breeches, and golf-stockings of John Hanford, the jewelled Parisian hood and pulled-about hair of his wife, are eloquent of the pride of these fatcats, and it would be as easy as invidious to contrast the gravity and distinction of Woolas with the ideal homes of Edgbaston.

A circuit of Bredon includes two churches of more than parochial interest—Bredon and Beckford. Both have those Norman features which we have remarked before as common in this southern pocket of our area ; Bredon can go still further back, for a monastery, founded by Eanulf, grandfather of Offa, is known to have been here before 716. The church (99), though almost dwarfed by the wonderful tithe barn of this village, has west and south arches of the best Norman ornament, and a north porch with chamber above. The roof, steeply pitched, is of open truss-work resting on corbel tables, and the tower is capped by one of the rare spires of south Worcestershire. A tomb, *c.* 1560, of William and Katherine Reed is curious for the inclusion, rare at this time, of a representation on the arch-moulding of the Deity appearing in clouds. The Mytton Chapel at Bredon contains

one of the few examples in England of the " heart burial "—
the inclusion, that is, of a heart held in the hand of the effigy,
and indicating that this part alone of the body is buried there.

[*Drawn by R. & J. A. Brandon*

99 BREDON CHURCH FROM THE SOUTH-WEST

The glory of Beckford is its remarkable tympanum, which
combines the motifs of " Christ in Glory " (found also at Ped-
more and Stockton in Worcestershire) and of " Good Over-
coming Evil " ; this latter theme recurs at Ribbesford, a mile

N

below Bewdley, and is here the whole subject of the composition. Good, a hunter with bow-and-arrow, is opposed by a curious monster, shaped much like a beaver but able to support itself on a broad fin-like tail.

From all this it will appear that the church-visitor, however single his purpose, must lead a very disordered life, continually bounding off at a rumour, unable to plan for more than one visit ahead. Suppose, however, that he chose to make a round of monastic fragments ; these, if we except the Cistercian remnants at Combe, Stoneleigh, and Merevale, and the Premonstratensian heap at Halesowen, amount to the Malverns, Pershore, Evesham, and Worcester, a company almost as compact as that of the five half-timbered towers at Pirton (100), Warndon, Dormston, Kington, and Cotheridge, none of which is more than nine miles from the county town.

[Drawn by W. A. Forsyth, F.R.I.B.A.

100   THE TOWER, PIRTON CHURCH,
WORCESTERSHIRE

The Malverns are best approached from Herefordshire, swinging up the Ledbury road until, passing the homes of such divergent figures as Elizabeth Browning and Jenny Lind, one's ears begin to crackle and pop as they would above Sisteron, and suddenly the whole Severn plain is put like a dish before one's eyes (1, 32). There are many pictures by Wilson Steer of this plain, and it is easy to imagine, in the foreground, one of the trailing Edwardian groups from which he leads the eye across to Bredon ; they are flying a kite, perhaps, or making an elaborate tea ; and the white

The Chained Bible and Sword Rest, All Saints, Worcester

The Lectern, Norton

Tiles, Gloucester Cathedral

A Misericord (The Judgment of Solomon), Worcester Cathedral

The Font, Castle Frome

102 A HAMLET CHURCH OF THE SEVERN PLAIN, CORSE,
GLOUCESTERSHIRE

103 LITTLE MALVERN PRIORY

hat or stockings of one pick out what is our own immediate concern—the priory of Little Malvern. This was a cell of the greater Malvern Priory, founded for seclusion and quiet living, rebuilt about 1480, and consisting now of tower, chancel, and presbytery; thus here, as at Evesham and Pershore, the fragments are properly fragments, and the " dismal hollow " of which Camden spoke is the prettier for this tiny building (103). Inside it has some curious late fifteenth-century glass, with royal portraits, some good woodwork, and inside the panelled belfry is a hiding-hole, a sanctuary

[Drawn by the Rev. J. L. Petit

104 HANLEY CASTLE CHURCH FROM THE SOUTH-EAST

within a sanctuary, against inquiring agents. Thus early in our tour, and in this most peaceful place, is raised the whole problem of the Reformation—how much was lost, and how much gained, by this reversion of power and property? I cannot help feeling that a certain displacement of emphasis might be useful to this controversy, and yet it is difficult to resist such a catalogue as is given by Dugdale of Thomas Cromwell's pillage at Warwick. " A part of the Cross," we learn, " was removed, some of the hair, milk, and raiment of the Virgin, part of the tomb of Christ, a thorn from the Head, part of the chair of Abraham, and part of the burning bush." I should like, nevertheless, to discover if more was not lost in the gradual progress, more thoughtless than fanatical, through the doldrums preceding the Oxford Movement, than in all the roaring 'forties of the Reformation. Anyone, meanwhile, who is delighted by Little Malvern (and that must be nearly everyone) can have a similar pleasure at Mathon, a few miles the other side of the hills ; here also is a timber roof of the fourteenth century, and a peal of bells, cast at Gloucester in 1760 ; excellent, however, as these are said to be, their sound has now to be taken on trust. Re-turning over the hills, and noting again the perfection of the fourteenth-century windows on the north and south of Little Malvern, we come into view of Malvern Priory Church. The late Perpendicular tower of this looks very well from above (32), and is a forecast of the climax reached at Gloucester by this opulent, even portly, style (86, 131). The church combines, in fact, the Norman and Perpendicular tendencies which we have found elsewhere—Norman in the stout piers, similar to but much shorter than those of Tewkesbury, and the plain three-ordered arcade ; Perpendicular in the great east window, the tall clerestory windows, and the abundance of fifteenth-century glass, some of it the gift of Richard III. Few churches are better stocked ; seasonal misericords, encaustic tiles, monuments of Crusaders and Tudor magnates, make pardonable the complacence of this town. Being of an indolent turn, I was delighted to turn up a letter of Charles Ricketts to Sydney Cockerell in which he says of Malvern : " It is a pleasant place situated in really fine country with character and feature. The Priory church . . . boasts three huge windows of fifteenth-century stained glass, in part harlequin, but not all, the upper part of the choir windows are entire, and there is a series of charming windows of the same date in the St. Anne Chapel . . . full of narrative force and exceptional character, they would have delighted Madox Brown. The colour throughout is singularly silvery, mostly white and blue with patches of dark red, violet, and olive, and of quite unusual quality for its epoch." [1]

Pershore, a most beautiful and neglected town (114), retains, of its Abbey church, only the tower, resembling that at Salisbury, and the Early English quire (107). At Evesham there is still less ; only the Bell Tower (94), an elaborate late Perpendicular building, and a rough archway leading

[1] *Letters to S.C.C.*, edited by Viola Meynell. Jonathan Cape. 1941.

[*Drawn by C. E. Mallows, F.R.I.B.A.*

105 GLOUCESTER QUIRE

formerly to the chapter house, are standing. Both, however, are eloquent survivals; the magnificence of the one, the austerity of the other, alternately witness to this departed way of life. At Evesham there is an element of panache which penetrates even to the coronets which crown its weather-vanes; and at Pershore the abbey is, from its very incompleteness, a perfect example of the column-and-vault

[*Drawn by H. D. Walton*

106 TWO BAYS OF PER-
SHORE ABBEY QUIRE

essential of Gothic. The balancing of the load, a dominant problem in Athens and Syracuse, had ceased to preoccupy builders; and no one can understand such a building as Pershore who does not imaginatively seize this great triumph—the elevation at will of enormous masses. Erich Mendelsohn, one of the most gifted of living architects, recognises only one more recent achievement; "the first iron girder," he says, "inspired an exalted feeling of liberation akin to that which the medieval masters felt when they had conquered the antique principle of construction by means of the vault."

Let us, while on this constructional tack, pass to Gloucester rather than to Worcester, for Gloucester, as well as being more monastic, follows more logically, as a fabric, than Worcester upon Evesham and Pershore. Nothing at Pershore is more beautiful than those alterations made necessary by the fires of 1223 and 1288; to these we owe, for instance, the five bays of that West of England Early English which originated at Wells and is found also in rather embryonic form in two bays of the nave at Worcester; and the open wooden roof of the presbytery was in its turn replaced by the late Decorated vaulting, the shafts running

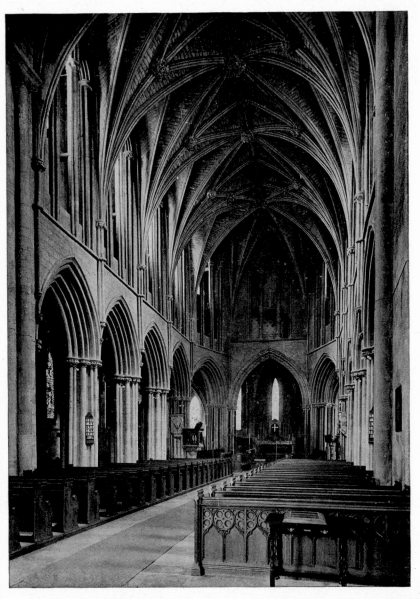

107 THE THIRTEENTH-CENTURY QUIRE OF PERSHORE ABBEY

108 MONUMENT TO THOMAS RUSSELL, STRENSHAM

apart and together above the united triforium and clerestory
(106, 107). This ploughshare vaulting with its huge sculptured
bosses, some as much as a yard in width and hiding many
beasts and monsters among their foliage, and the Lantern
Tower itself, damaged by the addition to its pinnacles in
1871 but still perfect below, worthily forecast the triumph
of a later age. For Gloucester also was mauled by fire. First,
in 1122, and again in 1300, occasion arose for rebuilding;
the great pillars of the nave still bear the mark of the earlier
blaze, and the monks' vaulting of the nave in 1242 replaced
the former wooden roof; in the south transept, the future
brilliance of the Perpendicular style was announced in 1330.
The Norman carcass of this great church is overlaid with
particular effect in the quire (105); and an observer stationed
beneath the organ-screen may apprehend, almost in a single
stride, the full achievement of this fourteenth century, for
before him will be the east window which, not less than the
Crécy it partly commemorates, resounds to the glory of
England. It is at such moments that an itinerist is most aware
of his deficiencies, and wishes for someone, at once architect
and poet, combining accurate observation with imaginative
speech. Such a one, in this case, is not sought in vain, for
Thomas Hardy, himself an architect before he became a poet,
has spoken of this sight. "Enter Gloucester," he says,

> " seek the quoin
> Where choir and transept interjoin,
> And, gazing at the forms there flung
> Against the sky by one unsung—
> The ogee arches transom-topped,
> The tracery-stalks by spandrils stopped,
> Petrified lacework—lightly lined
> On ancient massiveness behind— "

and notice also that this perfection is as great in little as all
the thirty yards height of the quire; for the very brilliant
and sophisticated canopy above the tomb of Edward II. is as
much an epitome of building tradition as are the cloisters. The
cloisters of Gloucester Cathedral are (if a little plunging may
be forgiven) very nearly the most beautiful piece of accessory
ecclesiastical architecture in England, and one must wonder at
a century which, working well inside its limits, produced these
cloisters, this quire, this monument, and this east window.
Gloucester was one of the houses least harmed by the Reformation; a census later revealed that every one of its former

friars was a stipendiary of some church in the diocese; it is as if the monastic system, having justified itself in each century, were given honourable retirement. For the fifteenth century in this cathedral is as fine as its predecessor, and the building which is rooted in Norman and bedecked with Perpendicular attains, in this little promontory of the Lady Chapel, such a sentiment of graciousness and farewell as attaches to some famous speeches in *The Tempest*.

There are other things at Gloucester; there is the Morley monument of Flaxman, the Hellenist who, alone among British sculptors, has been made the hero of a tract; but Flaxman, though given in his dotage to pietistic sentiments (he considered many drawings of Fuseli " shockingly indelicate "), and being, in his deformity, an object for compassion, was nevertheless, like many sculptors, a sly old cock, and Haydon gives this account of him at his devout period : " his old, deformed, humped shoulders protruded as he leant, and his sparkling old eye and his apish old mouth grinned on one side as he rattled out of his throat, husky with coughing, a jarry, inward, hesitating, hemming sound." There is also a great quantity of art-work by such nineteenth-century champions as Preedy, Hardman, Parry, and that curious team, Clayton and Bell—two names no more easily considered apart from each other (if we are to flatter them) than those of Liddell and Scott. And there is a wooden effigy of the middle twelfth century to Robert Curthose, son of the Conqueror. But it is the fabric and not the fittings which astound, and it is the last view of the Cathedral tower and its repeated pinnacles which illustrate for ever in the mind the definition of Gothic as " infinity made imaginable " (86, 131).

Gloucester to Worcester, by land or water, is not so far that we may not stop by the way. Strensham, it is true, is not strictly on our route, for it is on nobody's route, and no one goes there by accident. Once through the two gates, however, and down through the laurels to get the key, even a traveller uninterested in churches would be amused by the site of this small yet spacious church, to all appearances shut away among meadow grass, but in fact on a promontory overlooking the Avon and visible without glasses from the Malverns. There is the curious shape of the church (4), which has a broad aisleless nave and a tower broader than it

109 INTERIOR OF PRINCE ARTHUR'S CHANTRY, WORCESTER
CATHEDRAL

110 LOOKING TOWARDS THE SCENE OF THE BATTLE OF EDGEHILL

111 A WARWICKSHIRE LANE IN THE FOREST OF ARDEN DISTRICT

is long, that in its strong simplicity, bold stair-turret, and general effect inevitably recalls the achievements of Kent. Within is the rood-screen, turned into a gallery-front and containing twenty-four painted panels—twelve apostles, two kings, two archbishops, two bishops, and four saints ; this is one of those treasures whose mere existence is their chief claim to notice, for while the panels will not bear individual examination, yet the effect of the whole is good, and plays off excellently against the fine oak of the seating. There are five armoured brasses, of 1375, 1405, 1502, and 1556; and now that we are in this lonely place, and have our rubbers safely on their knees, it seems a good time to broach the whole question of sculpture. Facing us are the Russell monuments, a rare body of work, equalled only at Hanbury and Croome ; they represent a continuity in English taste which made possible the evolution of a style as eloquent, thoughtful, and allusive as that of the Francis Russell monument which we illustrate (6). It was (and this is often forgotten) in no sense a conservative, formal style ; it clung as closely as a shadow to its time. It used contemporary dress, and Roubiliac, for instance, fell for this reason under the *ex cathedra* condemnation of Reynolds ; if Roman dress were used, it was a symbol of immortality rather than a muffling convention. It adapted itself to all new adventures ; the pineapple and the turning globes of the Thomas Russell monument (108) and the three-masted sailing ship at Birtsmorton show that this was the time of Ralegh and Mercator ; the monument, which in Tudor times had often been a kind of popular show for outlying villagers, became a barometer lodged in the sensibility of its time, uniting Wesley and Chesterfield in its praise. Rysbrach, again, did not merely make a bust of Locke for Christchurch, Oxford—he equated himself with Locke ; Queen Caroline was regularly in his studio, and the reviews liked nothing better than stone-breaker's gossip. (The sixteenth issue of the *Spectator* is given over to Roubiliac.) Yet nothing of this attitude persists ; instead of that curious cachet which attaches to rubbers, the amateur of sculpture is aware, from the start, of a stigma. It is not, perhaps, unkindly meant ; it is not as if one had, on entering the church, been seen to be tipsy ; it is a kind of moral hiccough. I fancy it is that sculpture is a strenuous pleasure, and that Johnson had the root of it when he said, " The value of statuary

o

is in its difficulty ; you would not value the finest head cut on a carrot." Just as this difficulty makes many sculptors men of uneven temper, generously roused and full of caprice, so some part of it is communicated to the observer. Henry Moore, the most distinguished of living English sculptors, has said of amateurs that " although they may attain considerable accuracy in the perception of flat forms, they do not make the further intellectual and emotional effort needed to comprehend form in its full spatial existence." Sculpture is not easy going, and even such amiable habits as the cinema, or absorption in the printed page, work against that instinctive understanding of three dimensions which is the essential of this study. Let us therefore, and although it means abandoning the priestly station and Edwardian apparatus of the rubber, look specially at these unpopular beauties, whether here at Strensham, or at Brockley or Chesterton or Leamington Hastings—all places out of the way, yet each as exciting as Mistra or Monreale.

Church-visiting is mostly Anglican, but there is one tiny place of worship in this area which is not Anglican, is supported by no very large institution, but which is yet as beautiful as anything one could wish. This is the chapel at Worcester of the Countess of Huntingdon's Connection. Never a prominent or conspicuous building, it is now buried behind a new police station, and can be reached by only the most determined of its admirers. Methodism, of which Newman said, "never was a heresy mixed up with so much of what was good and true, so much high feeling and honest exertion," took excellent root in our area, for this has ever been anxious to make trial of recusant systems : first the Lollards, of whom a great many were at Coventry ; always, as we have seen, there has been an ultramontane party ; Bishop Roger of Worcester supported Becket against his king ; Charles I. complained of Anabaptists, Antinomians, Brownists, and Quakers ; in 1646 the cure of Kidderminster fell to Richard Baxter. Nor was the established church indifferently supported, and Hough and Stillingfleet were admirable men ; but in the 1760s Wesley went much about the fields of Worcestershire, finding the people " all of one heart and mind, so lovingly and closely united I have scarcely seen the like in the kingdom." Itinerant preachers, speaking in the fields, from tree-tops, or in quarries, produced no new phenomena in architecture, and little remains of this period but some pretty lettering above many a Worcestershire alley-mouth. Selina Huntingdon, however, had an appetite for building, and being at once a rich, personable widow, and a convert to Methodism, a patron of the Wesleys and of White-field, Venn, Romaine, and Toplady, it came easily to her to found a sect. Herself a Supralapsarian, she admitted Arminians and winked at Universalists; and though Southey hints that she was insane, she caused an agreeable stir in quarters not usually moved by such endeavours, and left for us such enchanting tabernacles as this and the one (paid for with her own jewels) at Brighton.

Walking along the waterfront, or up those narrow hill-streets which, with their recurring sight of one or other of Worcester's Renaissance churches, give to this county town an almost Italian savour, one reaches the Cathedral.

Few acts so discredit the Puritans' cause as the attempted destruction of Gloucester and Worcester Cathedrals; and the attempt, halted at Gloucester when instruments were ready for the disintegration of tower and lady-chapel, pro-ceeded at Worcester as far as the removal of glass and roof. Most of the fabric had to be restored (and this is a fact often ignored by those who follow the genteel convention of deploring all such repairs—that without them the fabric would often have fallen in, or required grotesque and con-tinuous propping) between 1857–74, and the Early English portion (that east of the tower) is its chief structural beauty. Of monastic work there is little beyond some detached ruins at the west end, the chapter-house, and the crypt. These and the two west bays (Transitional, and of green Highley sand-stone) of the nave contrast with the rest of the fabric; the crypt, with its seven apsidal bays, is prettily groined, and in it are preserved the ancient north doors of the cathedral. The sinister element proper to crypts is provided by the fact that these doors are covered with human skin, and it would be easy, wandering among the pillars of this sixpenny treat, to imagine oneself near the very similar chamber at Con-stantinople, about whose thousand columns there laps a limitless underground sea. The chapter-house has no such exotic pleasures; but about its mighty central pillar, a fitting pendant to the late Norman style of which we have seen so many triumphs, and throughout the whole of this decagon there is the heady smell of chapter politics, the constant awareness which attracted to the chapter library its books printed by Caxton and the manuscript of Vacarius on Roman Law. Moving through the cloisters, a hard-wearing Perpendicular square, one passes a stone, erected to the memory of an inconsolable Jacobite and inscribed " Miserrimus." To this Wordsworth composed an apostrophe ; but for it, no more than for Byron's " Verses found in a Summer-house at Halesowen," have we room.

Worcester Cathedral is beautifully kept, and the light, rebounding ceaselessly among its many vistas, takes from the stone a greenish colour until one could imagine oneself under the sea—in that cathedral, perhaps, of which Debussy and Breton legend have made a recurring image in the minds of many. Within this aquarium are the tombs of many who would not otherwise come to mind in combination. King John, for instance, though not much thought of nowadays, was very fond of this area, and regularly kept Christmas in it, liking the food, liking the hunting, going much in awe of Bishop Wulstan, and liking most of all to go visiting among his wealthier subjects ; and this great week-ender chose to be buried at Worcester in the company of St. Wulstan. Buried he was, but soon he was moved to his present position in the quire ; this is the earliest royal effigy in England, but whereas the tomb of Edward II. attracted pilgrims in sufficient number to finance the re-building of Gloucester, King John brought little revenue, and in 1218 the tithes of Grafton Manor were assigned to the upkeep of lights about his tomb.

Not all those who lie here do so by design. In the south aisle, and a little intimidated by its Norman rigour, is a monument to Richard Solly, who died at Malvern in 1803, " seized with an inflammation of the intestines while on a tour of Pleasure with his family." There are many beautiful tombstones of this period in our area, but a composition on this scale, with widow, coffin, and three children in their best, is normally an embarrassment ; here, however, it is enchanting, and this generation, that of Schubert and Tom Moore, comes off a second time in the nearby Cazalet monument. Such private griefs, however, yield before the national loss of which Prince Arthur's chantry is the monument ; this elder brother of Henry VIII., endowed with the precocious sweetness and poetic allure of many early Tudor characters,

lies within an elaborate late Gothic tomb of which the tracery
and the beautiful *enchaînement* of figures on the east wall of
the interior run in with the lady-chapel of Gloucester as the
last champions of pre-Reformation building in this area (109).

There are several good and honest but rather dour seventeenth-century family tombs at Worcester;   there is Bishop
Thornborough, the alchemist, who died in 1641 ; and the
Moore monument of 1613 musters three husbands and their
wives, and beneath the fan-vaulting of their canopy these
wives astonish us by wearing each a copy of the *chapeau
important* of Baudelaire.   In the south transept, and wasting
a remarkable site, is a monument by Brock of Bishop Phill-
pott, who died in 1890 ; this is a case in which the primary
criterion of sculpture—that it should be more important
than the air which it displaces—is not met.   Chantrey, though
not approaching the sentimental height (for which, indeed,
at least a marquisate was required) of his Hertford tomb at
Alcester, does very well with his Mrs. Digby, a product of
the period when this bottle-nosed, snuff-taking, arrogant old
fox was relaxing from his triumph at Lichfield.   The lady-
chapel arcading and aisles are filled with a variety of medieval
sculpture which, taken together, ignoring most of the ascrip-
tions and some modern additions to the arcades, is a remarkable corpus of work ; it will be several hundred years before
we shall see either the nervous, eliminating line of the lying
figures or the quality of mind, quick and clear as an exposition
of Cæsar, behind the narrative upon the walls.   It will not,
in fact, be till 1746, when the Hough monument of Roubiliac
was finished.   This was an early work of Roubiliac, done
before his visit to Italy ; yet it recalls us at once to a great
European tradition, for this Huguenot and Gascon had been
the pupil of Balthasar Permoser, sculptor of the Zwinger
Pavilion at Dresden, and later of Nicholas Couston, the Rome
prizewinner of 1676 and author of the " Descent from the
Cross " in Notre Dame.

Bishop Hough was a man of exceptional wisdom and
energy, to whom we owe, for instance, the re-building of
the diocesan palace at Hartlebury.   This building, standing
in an estate whose infertility caused it to be given over to
deer and guinea-pigs, had been dismantled on surrender to
the Parliamentarians, and Hough, though tempted to exchange
it for a half-timbered house in the vicinity, finally built the

red-sandstone, battlemented palace now existing. This charming house is a tribute to the enlightenment of the best Anglican tradition, for Bishop Hurd gave the library (much of which had belonged to Pope) and Stillingfleet laid out in the park an avenue of limes. During the Napoleonic invasion scare it was proposed that George III., in the event of a landing, should find asylum at Hartlebury, and both it and its counterpart (now the Deanery) at Worcester are uncommonly pleasant perquisites.

The Hough monument is the most important single composition in our area, and the figure of the Bishop reclining in his robes is an astonishing advance upon previous monumental schemes. It is not improper here to use a military metaphor and speak of the organisation in depth, the use of every inch of recession, which marks this off from other work ; the relief, in which Hough is shown pleading the case of the Fellows of Magdalen who upheld against James II. their right to elect their President for themselves, is an eighteenth-century development paralleled at Worcester in the adjoining Maddox monument (a tropical fantasy) and in the Waterloo scene, over in the south aisle, of John Bacon's Ellis monument ; Warwickshire has earlier examples, and till recently there could be seen at Coventry the Nethermyl monument with its endless municipal rites. At Charlecote there is a first-class Shakespearian relic in the monument by Schurman to Sir Thomas Lucy ; this, in form a three-arched canopy on four black marble columns, contains two effigies, and on one side of them a representation of Sir Thomas' library, with Homer, Cato, Vergil and his journal, and on the other a relief of him riding through his park—this is, in fact, the only representation of the park as it was in the poet's time.

It would be difficult, after the great water-spouting line of these two cathedrals, to return to humbler Gothic ; let us, therefore, omitting the civic churches until a later occasion, consider what is rarely considered—the private church or chapel of the eighteenth century, typified here at Croome (5, 112), at Compton Verney, at Honington (129), and at Compton Wynyates. (There is also a church after Adam at Binley, which I have not been able to see.)

Mr. Goodhart-Rendel once chose the chapel of Compton Wynyates, rebuilt in 1663, as the type of " planning by subdivision "—as against the " building by aggregation "—of which the house is the supreme example. It is in any case a very modest, elegant building, ornamented simply by hatchments, a number of broken monuments fished from the lake in which they were thrown by Roundheads, and a curious painting of "Day and Night"; the altar is three-sided and without reredos, while the centre of the church is filled by four great box-pews. This formal, clean-smelling church is completed by a row of family banners.

At Compton Verney the chapel is of a hundred years later and even more urbane; old Italian glass has been put in some of its windows, and to the monument by Nicholas Stone (1630) two early sixteenth-century brasses have been added from the former Benedictine chapel; there is of 1668 a very dashing tomb by Edward Hurst with white busts and figures of "Labour" and "Rest"; and in the windows, scenes from the life of St. Catherine of Siena, brought in the early seventeenth century from Italy, have as companions English family groups of a century earlier. Honington is more public, although from its churchyard, thickly inlaid with buttercups, one can see the sham ruin in the garden of the Hall, and an unwary departure from the church will bring one sharply beneath the Emperors enthroned around the house. A Renaissance church of the late seventeenth century (129), it has a tower whose lower stage is of the thirteenth; there is much fine woodwork among the pulpit, the altar rails, and choir seating, and a pew for children of the family; but the west end is dominated by a large canopied platform on which two enormous figures in early eighteenth-century dress strut and parade like tenors at a benefit; it is galling in war-time to come on two men so sumptuously fed.

Croome Church was not the only resort of those who lived in the court, for, long before the present church was built in 1763, a chapel was established in one of the upper rooms of the house. The present church stands well up on a hill, overlooking the house and its stables, the demesne and the distant prospect invented by Brown; sometimes when hounds meet at Croome, the hunt comes through the precinct of the church (112), and the winter sunshine throws up, as upon a screen, the civil pageantry of the chase. Neither fabric nor interior (5) may be safely ascribed to Adam, but the wooden font, for instance, and the coving of the ceiling, seem to speak for him.

This post-Renaissance brought many accessories to existing churches, and it is fascinating to sniff out such additions as make of Preston-on-Stour, for example, a kind of Gothic *salon*. The chancel of this was rebuilt by West in 1752 ; the chalice font is dated 1747 ; the chalice and paten, 1750. It is approached through a leafy tunnel of yews, entered through pretty Georgian gates. The glass in the chancel consists partly of early seventeenth-century Dutch grisailles, partly of work contemporary with its rebuilding ; and the dedication of this to " the universal dominion of death " recalls one sharply to the hatred of shams which, natural enough in an area not given to perfunctory belief, comes out again in such inscriptions as this, from Bromsgrove :

> " Encomiums on the dead are empty sounds and mockery ; the last great day alone will wipe the colouring off, and man's true state, without a veil, will stand disclosed to view."

Eastlake, the first historian of the Gothic revival, selected 343 examples of its work, and of these ten occur in our area, six of them churches. On its own valuation, then, this period would wish to be judged by St. Chad's (the work of A. W. Pugin) and Thomas's St. Matthew's at Birmingham ; Woodyer's church, erected at the expense of, and garnished with paintings by, Gambier Parry at Highnam. Woodyer, a pupil of Butterfield and a devil for restoration, executed also St. Stephen's, at Redditch, and the church at Tenbury—both, to Eastlake's eye, distinguished work. The last and latest of these is one designed by Street at Toddington, and this, Eastlake concludes with awe, was erected " regardless of expense." Few towns, on this estimate, are as happy as Rugby, for not only has this an Anglican church by Butterfield, but also a Roman Catholic church, designed by the elder Pugin, enlarged by the younger. But in fact there is nothing which, more quickly than a tour of these expensive churches, attunes one's eye to the authentic in English building and sends one into lonely places—places deserted, perhaps, like Chesterton, by the enclosure of fields four centuries ago ; or into places like Kinwarton, with its few fragments of fourteenth-century glass ; Mitcheldean, with its Norman font and twelve Apostles sculptured on it ; or most of all, into such a mixture as the church at Leamington Hastings. This has the embattled pinnacled tower of Warwickshire in the

112 THE CROOME HUNT IN CROOME CHURCHYARD

113 COVENTRY : after the raid

114 GEORGIAN ROOFS, PERSHORE

115 VICTORIAN RESIDENCES, GREAT MALVERN

fifteenth-century, with bizarre figures grinning from its string-courses; its chancel was rebuilt about 1670; the fourteenth-century south aisle has a large corbel table, with masks; entering by the north door, we at once see in this a fine example of early Decorated, with bold naturalistic ornament—leaves, fruit, and tendrils depending from the open mouths of masks; the font, of the early fifteenth century, is panelled and has angelic figures; there is an old chest, a collection of gloves, swords, helmets, and other curiosa; and

115A OLD CHARLECOTE CHURCH, now rebuilt in
ornate modern Decorated

here, with the piscina and the chamfered arch and the dagger from Edgehill, are two monuments by John Bushnell, an artist whose paranoia was developed to proportions which, even in a sculptor, called for comment. These were small tasks after his Mocenigo monument in the church of the Mendicanti at Venice, for this, apart from a gigantic cornice with pillars and recessed pilasters, apart from the figures of the Virgin and of the chubby-legged, misshapen Procuratore, included two enormous reliefs, one (almost, it was said, life-size) of the siege of Candia, the other of a naval engagement between Venetians and Turks. They were trifling even against the Trojan Horse which he constructed for a wager; this was large enough for twelve men to sit inside it, using its

P

eyes as windows, and was of timber, with the muscles of the head picked out in stucco. This he sold for £500 to a vintner who wished to use it as a tavern ; but one day a gust of wind caught it broadside and toppled it in pieces. No such insubstantial vision are these two bold and spirituous pieces, and it is upon the dynamic male heads (Bushnell could make only insipid female heads, and could not make a nude of any kind, but all his men are dragons) that our eyes rest in imagination as the train draws us southwards, towards the blue Cotswolds, towards the cuckoo-echoing city of Oxford, and out of the Shakespeare country.

[*Drawn by Arthur Stratton, F.S.A., F.R.I.B.A.*

115B THE SAXON FONT, DEERHURST CHURCH

117 MONTPELLIER TERRACE

CHELTENHAM

116 TREILLAGE VERANDAHS

118 CHELTENHAM, BELOW ITS ENCIRCLING HILLS

119 CARVING IN CHESTERTON CHURCH

CHAPTER

VI

TOWN AND COUNTRY

THIS is mild country, with nothing monstrous in it; a little to the west there is the Forest of Dean with its haunted collieries; a little to the south there are the bleak Cotswold moors; go but a little way in any direction and you will find mountain torrents, desolate spaces, and people speaking other tongues; but in our own country there is nothing more terrible than the slow turning of the wheel beside the mill at Shipston; no one freezes to death on the Malverns. It is a land-lock, living apart from the sound of the sea; it is wonderfully suggestive country, and it is in despair of conveying its quality that one quotes a great connoisseur of our civilisation: "Warwickshire," says Henry James, " is the core and centre of the English world; midmost England, unmitigated England."

Most people would enter Warwickshire from the south, travelling whether by train or road within sight of Edge Hill. Edge Hill is one of the indecisive battles of the world, and indeed, by the standards of Smolensk or the Marne, was hardly a battle at all—a day-excursion, let us say, with some

123

fighting thrown in. At the top of the hill, an excellent place
of vantage, is an octagonal tower, put up in 1750 by Sanderson
Miller. Richard Jago, who from his rectory at Harbury could
easily have walked over and back in a day, remarked its

> " broken arch
> And mould'ring wall, well taught to counterfeit
> The waste of Time."

But the tower to-day has no need of counterfeit, and is as
battered as anyone could wish. Much of the land has been
enclosed since 1642, and the steep western side of the hill
laid under cultivation (110) ; but for all that it is easy to
imagine the royal forces in line from Nadbury to Sunrising,
and up in the trees above Burton Dassett the pickets spying
out the little army of Parliament as it came out from Kineton
to the plain. Between them cantered one of the Shuckburghs,
out hunting with his hounds ; while in a thicket, a little
apart from the fighting ground, the two little sons of the
King lay stubbornly construing Vergil with a man who had
not long since discovered the circulation of the blood. Richard
Baxter preached that day at Alcester, on the text " The Kingdom
of Heaven suffereth violence," with the gunfire as an accom-
paniment to the sermon.

A mile or two from Edgehill is Warmington, a village
well up on the hill, with a church containing provision on
its north side, in the upper part of a two-storeyed erection,
for a resident priest, but remarkable mostly for the great
pond about which its houses cluster. This is one of the
villages least affected by enclosure ; elsewhere in this lovely
and deserted area one constantly meets with isolated churches,
single barns, and such lonely relics as the mill and beacon on
Burton Dassett Hill. At Farnborough, nearby, the rectory
is a very good seventeenth-century minor domestic building.

But this is hill country, in which an unwary turn of the
head will bring into view any one of twelve counties ; pushing
a little northwards into Warwickshire one comes into more
local country, now undulant and peppered with elms, but at
other times observably flat, and showing in its regular striping
the intensity of war-time cultivation. Only at the very border
of the roads is there a spirit of peace-time *laissez-aller*, and
one can run for miles, either by random lanes (111) or along
the Roman road which, straight as those of Napoleon, cuts
off this corner from the rest of the county, and never miss

120 PRESTON-ON-STOUR, WARWICKSHIRE

the long grass on either side. At Chesterton, as at Nadbury, there are Roman remains, but there are also English ones, and better. The windmill at Chesterton is well known; usually it is in empty country, and at present, if one troubles to make the climb and inspect its masonry, crumbling loft, and immovable sails (60), one's curiosity is suspect, for this is a sensitive part, and a traveller, at the end of a day's walking about it, begins to see a constable in every copse. But in peace-time there were annual point-to-points at Chesterton, and from the thistles at the windmill's base the whole pageant could be seen for nothing; it was plain from the rich colour of the turned earth, the profusion of natural fences and stretches of open turf, that this was excellent hunting country. It was always so, indeed, and from 1793 to 1812 the Warwickshire enjoyed a run as famous as any in the history of this amusement. A little way from this eminence, and looking towards the church, there is a watermill, living off a lake from whose borders rushes and celery and golden-dock advance towards the rumoured currents of its centre. Elsewhere in Warwickshire there are many streams on which a patient observer might hope to see the floating Ophelia; but this pool recalls an earlier story, for it is Arthurian, and anyone walking there will do well to weight his pockets with Tennyson or Malory.

Not far from this deserted water is Chesterton church, itself exposed upon a hill and far from its parishioners; in this are four Stuart busts to the Peyto family. Two of these are by Nicholas Stone; the others Mrs. Esdaile attributes to John Stone. Nothing could more conveniently distinguish art from craftsmanship than the way in which Nicholas Stone, by giving his busts a tiny inclination, and playing this off against the coving of his canopy, brings into play a whole series of relations unknown in the square elevation of John Stone. The busts are no better; it is just that more is made of them.

This country east of the Fosse Way, with its memories of battle and melancholy vistas of waving grass, comes oddly enough in our area; and so equally does the district a little to the south. These " blue Cotswolds " are not admitted by Mr. Massingham to be true children of the parent range, but myself I am strongly for these curious humps (some of them almost as freakish as the hills of Le Puy), and many of the villages, with their clean-swept north Cotswold stone, have something of the snap and excitement of towns that live within sight of the sea. Brailes, for instance; even the name is trimmed against the weather, and the great tower which causes this church to be called "the Cathedral of the Feldon" is a wiry, stubborn affair, for all the five lights of its west window. But at Barcheston, an hour's walk away, there is already the indulgent, sloping Warwickshire tower. The moral outlook of the Cotswolds is quickly lost; not so its material and style. At Tredington, two miles from Shipston, there is still a Cotswold spire of the loveliest kind (121); and at Honington, for all the seclusion of its muffling elms, there

[*Drawn by Sydney R. Jones*

121   TREDINGTON, WARWICKSHIRE

are still a good many small houses of Cotswold stone. Honington is the most exquisite of Warwickshire villages, but everywhere in this overbred, park-like country there are, if not whole villages, at any rate a few houses in every village with something of the same urbanity; at Ettington, for instance, there is a breath-taking eighteenth-century house in the middle of the village. In this respect also, the area knows no neutral country, and one passes without warning into the empire of Midland brick. This is not absolutely true, and such charming villages as Barford, for example, in which the agitator, Joseph Arch, was born, include many cottages in this

122 THE TEME VALLEY, NEAR STANFORD

123 THE SEVERN VALLEY FROM NEAR EASTNOR

124 NEAR STANFORD, LOOKING TO THE CLEE HILLS

125 THE WORCESTERSHIRE TEME VALLEY
A close-up of a wooded hill stretch

brick which are as cooling to the eye as the Avon by which they stand.   Turning up east from Barford one comes to another unnatural stretch of country.   Dunsmore Heath is a deserter from the rest of Warwickshire; it is a low plateau, keeping all its treasures near the ground, excepting perhaps the avenue of elm and fir along the old high road from London to Birmingham—excepting, too, the British camp on Knightlow Hill.   It is barbarous country, and fittingly introduces us to Rugby.

Rugby Station is an ember-coloured effort in that L.M.S. Railway manner which is consummated at St. Pancras; Dickens disliked it and turned it into " Mugby Junction," but if one is familiar with the mythology of railway stations (and few scenes of modern life are more fruitful in legend) then this is a goodish one, and it would be amusing to see it in a Hitchcock film. Once outside the station one has a galaxy of associations from which to choose.   Scott and Street, it is true, Bodley and Butterfield, Pugin and

[*From " Tom Brown's Schooldays "*

126 RUGBY CLOISTERS

Pugin, have worked on this town; but it is also a town in which Rupert Brooke wrote and Wystan Auden was born. Let us, however, and with our ears plugged against this pair of sirens, proceed to Rugby School.

No one in our time but Mr. G. M. Young has fairly taken the measure of Thomas Arnold.   Enlightened opinion (which could not turn more regularly if it were roasted on a spit) has come to accept the son; but of the father no newer aspect has been brought securely into view than that introduced by

Lytton Strachey in the final summer of an earlier war. Yet the Arnolds, like the Stephens and the Toynbees and the Frys, were in a sense our own begetters ; remorseless as Hannibal and unobtrusive as the London Library, they made sure that none of us can frame a sentence, judge a fellow-being, or make a decision for ourselves without unwitting reference to them. Arnold and Jowett between them trans-formed the higher education of an Empire ; and just as Jowett left nothing of the spirit of Bentley, Porson, and Grote, so there was no trace at Rugby of the humane illuminants who had so recently kept a school not thirty miles away.

The Hills were just such an inquisitive, energetic family as was the inheritance of many a late Victorian hero. It was not, as it often is with us, that from one great man descended a tribe of languid nobodies ; rather did each possess some new, inquiring virtue of his own. Thomas Wright Hill, the son of a horse-dealer, was an amateur astronomer, an " honest, guileless, unconventional " member of Mr. Priestley's con-gregation. Ruined by the French wars, he set up near Edg-baston as schoolmaster, proclaimed all knowledge to be of equal value, and within a few years had sent out from his classes a future Master of Caius and a Professor of Greek in the University of Cambridge. His methods were liberal, and he kept few accounts, so that his sons, Rowland and Matthew, had soon to take over the books. Rowland was a dietician, a prodigy at mathematics, and a terrible reader of Maria Edgeworth, before he went to the Post Office. Matthew was a journalist, and the first Birmingham man to be a member of Lincoln's Inn. There were few who, arrested for blasphemy or rioting or some political offence, had not an advocate in Matthew Hill, and in 1822 he wrote his *Public Education*, in which something of that faith in the essential sanctity of human nature which was to irradiate the Clapham Sect, awoke response even in the castles of unbelief. Bentham read it with delight, and Mill ; but Arnold had no copy.

There is more to be said for Arnold than for his system. For a man gifted with absolute power over others, he used it with discretion, breaking out only in chapel. He took an almost Hegelian view of the world in which he was ruler, but he admitted that in " that great self," his school, there were many whose qualities would appear only in adult life. He was an unsparing crammer, and yet the carriages of that

smoking novelty, the railway train, were full of his pupils,
packed off on the " fifty miles' journey by rail," which he prescribed for all overworked systems. He was a partial, bigoted,
moralising interpreter; yet he brought, as Mr. Young says,
" science, scholarship, and political insight " into the empty
heads before him, and those whose fathers were opposing the
First Reform Bill were made free of the political life of Israel,
Greece, and Rome. And virtue, in the end, he respected less
than acumen. " The temptations of the intellect," he said,
" are not comparable to the temptations of dullness."

This formidable, unsettled, fecund usher was, moreover,
a person of some taste in landscape. At Rugby he com-

[*From " Tom Brown's Schooldays "*

127 THE ELMS, RUGBY

mented on " the unsurpassable dullness of the scenery:
nothing but one endless monotony of enclosed fields and
hedgerow trees." There is something of Leicestershire in it,
and it comes as no surprise that Tattersall's, even fifty years
ago, had a branch establishment in Rugby.

A little way from Rugby is Bilton. In the church are
brass chandeliers from Bois-le-Duc in Brabant, but it is the
Hall which is most interesting, for here Addison lived
from 1712 until his death in 1719, and here he brought his
wife, the Dowager Countess of Warwick. This neatest and
most affable of writers here planted with his own hands some
Spanish chestnuts given him by a friend, but the fine walk
into which they grew was unhappily destroyed some eighty
years later after his daughter's death. But there are dour parts,

Q

and it is by South Warwickshire that one most agreeably approaches the vitals of the area. Such a village as Ilmington, for instance, banked up on half a dozen shelving paths, thatched and cut across by tiny streams, is more to our purpose. Some of the low walls at Ilmington are themselves roofed with thatch ; and this, though it seems affected, is in fact a survival of Shakespeare's time, and Capulet's orchard-wall had just such a top covering of straw. The rectory of Ilmington is of Cotswold stone and is conspicuous even in this area of fortunate incumbents.

This is still stone country, and Shipston is mostly a stone town, excellently plain and with many large inns and open squares recalling the time when this was at once a market and a thoroughfare town. (One of its hotels had still, a year after Dunkirk, a remarkable cellar.) Its many pretty, square and bow-fronted windows look out upon a quieter scene, but Wesleyans still walk up their original alley, while Anglicans make do with a church whose chief ornament is a baby magnolia growing up its side. These are little towns of quality. Alcester, on the road in from Worcester, retains something of that éclat which followed the arrival, in the 1780s, of the famous physician Brandish. Conversation in the town at that time is said to have run on three main lines : the improvements effected at Birmingham, the excesses of the Parisian mob, and the pleasures of Twickenham. In 1803 a detachment of Home Guardsmen was recruited at Alcester, and there is an echo of July 1940 in this account of them : " little is talked of beside soldiering : they meet three afternoons a week and have a man from Birmingham to instruct them : their clothes are not yet made "—though these clothes (scarlet trimmed with yellow) are far enough from battle-dress. There were dances at Alcester, and Wakes (one July Sunday saw six), and there had till recently been cock-fighting ; but there was no theatre, and for this one had to go to a rough platform behind the " King's Head " at Worcester, on which an actress of a certain talent, called Mrs. Siddons, performed from time to time.

Alcester has kept its houses, and its Fish Saloon is prettier than many a great town house. Another house of the period has a front door, with full equipment, on the first floor, and behind the church there is a dazzling row of professional Regency beauties. Its town hall is earlier, of 1641, and similar

128 A BY-WAY IN ELMLEY CASTLE VILLAGE, WORCESTERSHIRE

129 HONINGTON CHURCH, WARWICKSHIRE

A Georgian composition with fine woodwork and monuments

130   THE SOUTHERN MALVERNS: CHASE END, RAGGEDSTONE, AND MIDSOMER HILLS

to that of Ledbury, except that the black-and-white upper part is carried upon stone and not upon chestnut.

The road from the Arrow valley to Stratford is, in appearance, one string of charming villages, each with a double front, one to the road and one, across gardens and churchyards and the irregular cut-waters of the Avon bridge, upon the river. Bidford and Welford and Wixford are all of this kind; but only leave the valley, and such anomalies are revealed as scattered Exhall, from whose roofs tiles are missing—as they are missed where mountain winds tug ceaselessly. Warwickshire needs watching: even the run-in to Stratford has its enterprise, when to the long, wooded avenue there suddenly succeeds the wilderness of outer Stratford.

This is still a play-town, and as such almost unique in war-time England. Many towns given over in peace-time to pleasure have now a new character; nothing could be more lovely than the empty, mined, and barricaded crescent of Weymouth Bay. But Stratford is unchanged. In the event this is just as well; the theatre, for instance, can never have been more welcome; not since W. B. Yeats lay in a deck-chair outside the earlier building and wrote an apostrophe to the spirit of the festival, can people have been so glad of the players in Shakespeare's town. The church, too, with the opulence of its tracery, the plump line of its chancel, and the Clopton chapel packed with the pride of lineage—there could not well be change in that. Even Gerard Johnson's bust, coloured by John Hall in 1748, painted out by Malone in 1793, painted in again by Simon Collins in 1861, may be spared further modification. The river-front of Stratford, the Clopton bridge, and the running Avon are obstinately beautiful; and many of its relics are unexpectedly stimulating. There is a good Rysbrack in the church, of 1751. The Cattermole series of Shakespearian water-colours is a charming piece of colloquial art. The town hall is of 1763 and has two Gainsboroughs, one Romney, a Hogarth, and Roubiliac's remarkable statue of Shakespeare, while throughout the town there are interesting houses of every period in which tourists, or the native assiduity in trade, have enriched the inhabitants. It remains a play-town, for all that half its hotels are boarded up; the shops are still full of folk-weave, and in one of them is concentrated rock from every forbidden watering-place in England. The Birthplace, which one would think to have been so frequented as to retain no more private quality than a railway waiting-room, has yet an irrepressible appeal. Something—it may be the names of Thackeray, Dickens, and Kean upon the wall, or that of Scott upon the window—sets one off : or perhaps it is simply the pleasure of pilgrimage. Elsewhere in the town are the remnants of the gallery of Shakespearian pictures planned by Boydell ; these are not the best paintings in this genre : they are not equal to Delacroix's " Portrait of the Artist as Hamlet," or to Fuseli's " Lady Macbeth." But they are interesting as a relic of this unhappy enterprise, and some of them (Reynolds' " Death of Cardinal Beaufort," *e.g.*, and Northcote's " Hubert and Prince Arthur ") are curious objects in themselves.

If Stratford is little affected by the war, Cheltenham has been restored to something of its original gaiety. Admittedly one house was destroyed by a casual bomb, but in other respects Cheltenham has not enjoyed such good spirits since in 1780 one Simon Moreau was appointed Master of those Ceremonies by which the visitors (in that year numbering 370) were diverted. It was forty-two years since a pump-room had been built at Cheltenham, and seventeen since elms had been planted in Well Walk. One handsome street still contained the whole town, and it was to be eight years before Moreau received the King and Queen. No sooner, however, was the visit over and Cheltenham implanted in the royal heart (so firmly, indeed, that he would accost strangers in Weymouth and ask for news of the town in which their faces had become familiar to him), no sooner had Badminton and Oakley, Croome and Hartlebury closed their doors upon the departing monarch, than Cheltenham began to build against a permanent increase of custom. Its population increased sixfold between that time and the beginning of work in Pittville in 1824 ; vetting was never relaxed, and each newcomer was on suspicion of being either an actor or a person engaged in retail trade. For those who passed this test there was every amenity. Between 1804–08, Montpellier Wells was put up " at almost incalculable expense," and the name of this quarter recalls the wine-wreathed formality of the town then much in favour with the English. Pittville, finished a generation later, ruled off in squares and shaded with lime and cedar, in some way recalls another part of France ; it is as if we were suddenly at Auteuil, and behind this green and yellow

shaded stucco there were the Seine, and instead of the Midland
Red the splashing water-omnibus. In point of fact, Pittville is
backed by the theosopher's quarter of Cheltenham. To this
graveyard of belief there has recently come a new supersti-
tion—next door to a vendor of kosher poultry there is a
temple of Jehovah's Witnesses. Unfortunately, these sects no
longer inspire such masterpieces of occasional architecture as
the Masonic building.

Early visitors to Cheltenham had many pleasures prepared
for the morning when they first walked beneath the ilices
and into the town itself. There was Duffield and Weller's
literary saloon; behind some anonymous window Lord
Byron was writing " The Corsair " ; at the Harp and Piano-
forte Warehouse they could secure the use of a double-action
harp by Erard and Dodd; there were shops between the
caryatids along Montpellier walk ; Jessop's Nursery Garden
could offer the study of " Student's beds upon the Linnæan
Model," or, safely within a hive of glass, the improving
diversion of the winged republic. Not everyone, however,
regarded the visitors with the eyes of Moreau, and for this
reason alone it would be discourteous to compare its original
to its present aspect. " There is certainly," said Selina
Huntingdon, " an incorrigible apathy about the gay who
frequent this place." This is not an entirely unamiable trait,
nor is it one which with the passage of time can be said to
have disappeared from Cheltenham. But Cobbett's account
is another matter ; hardly had he crossed the Avon and seen
this town set in the cornice of the hills before he burst with
spleen. It was " a place to which East India plunderers,
West India floggers, English tax-gorgers, together with
gluttons and drunkards and debauchers of all descriptions,
female as well as male, resort . . . in the hope of getting rid
of the bodily consequences of their manifold sins and in-
iquities." This is going far ; for the true colonial era was not
yet. And although I could not find, among those commemorated in Christ Church, a single one whose career was made in
England, these were honourable dim lives and apart from the
" gamesters, pickpockets, and harlots " with whom Cobbett
perforce kept company.

Cheltenham in a war-time summer is such a town as one
imagines Biarritz to have been forty years ago, one in which
one comes at every corner upon a Bulgarian diplomatist, a

woman leading an ape upon a chain, the brothers of an exiled monarch, or (in uniform) a high officer of an extinct Republican army. I have seen all these things in Cheltenham, and sensed others, inspired perhaps by the statue to King Edward VII., in which the Emperor, in golfing costume, faces the Promenade with his hand upon the head of a handsome child of unknown parentage. It is easy to imagine the westward confluence of visitors from Aix and Vichy and Baden-Baden, and to hear through the Pump Room doors the interruption of the number from the *Grande Duchesse de Gerolstein* by the national hymn —Tuscany it might be, Bohemia, or Brandenburg—of an additional monarch. There are more confusing treats in Cheltenham ; it is startling, for instance, to explore the quartz and antlers of the local museum and hit on a picture by Helleu, the artist whom Jacques Blanche identifies with the early Elstir of Proust. Here, in a back street of Cheltenham, one stumbles on a tiny incident in a painter's life, yet one akin to those greater incidents for which a roomful of Guermantes was kept from its dinner. Cheltenham is one with Blandford and Weimar and Dieppe, one of the little towns of European quality. She has already her inquiring admirers (Anthony West, for example, and Hugh Casson) ; I cannot think that she will not have more.

The war, which taps the barometer of every town, similarly explores the forgotten resources of the open country. Coming from Cheltenham towards Pershore one crosses one of the most lovely and enduring of all Avon bridges, standing irregularly among celandines. This masterpiece at Eckington is defended by a block-house, and each of the stones which compose it has shell-markings from a time before there were tyrants ; these are the surprises of war-time, known to those who reclaim inhospitable land or keep watch from the cupolas of ruined churches.

The Severn valley (123), whether down to Gloucester or up to Worcester, is dominated by the Malverns (32, 130). This is not a major range : its highest point can be reached in half an hour from the Winter Garden below ; its circuit could be made on foot between breakfast and dinner ; but in the emotional calculus of the valley it is as important as the river itself. It has nothing to match the " Severn smell " which Elgar attempted to capture in many of his works ; but it has a wonderful variety of light, alternately brilliant

131 GLOUCESTER: THE CATHEDRAL TOWER FROM MILLER'S GREEN

132 TWYNING FERRY, ON THE AVON

133 THE DOCKS AT GLOUCESTER

and sombre. It is best, perhaps, on a January morning, and seen from such a town as Upton (37), above whose narrow streets and high-pitched roofs the little range sparkles with frost, reflected sometimes in the ice on the intervening fields. The Alpine illusion is common also in the upper reaches of Cheltenham, where the encircling hillside is deep in snow and one might think oneself in Chambéry until one sees, between the laurels, the peeling maps of Africa and Asia, and the piled goloshes in the porch. Only at Gloucester itself are these hills forgotten; for this is, in feeling if not in fact, the first town in the West Country, at once more temperate and more seasoned than the Midlands, aware of the sea and of those who sail upon it. Admittedly most of the ships in Gloucester harbour are not barques but barges (133), and travel to nowhere more distant than Sharpness. Here is nothing fanciful; no sailor docks at Gloucester with, say, a ruby the size of a walnut in his pocket; and Westgate Street, for all its hundreds of verifiable workers, is nothing to the terraces of Odessa. Indeed (and although Murray remarks that around the docks are to be found many foreign flowers, of which the seeds were sown unwittingly by sailors returning from abroad) one might take the town on its own valuation as the original home of Sunday schools if it were not for the urgency, in war-time, of such homely traffic as fills and empties the wharves, and the shallow hooting boats beside them; or such surprises as the cavernous underground bar of the " Fleece," among whose glistening stones one might imagine enacted the " Lower Depths " of Gorki. In the Bell Inn at Gloucester, George Whitfield was born in 1714, and in St. Mary de Crypt he was baptized and preached his first sermon. Whitefield was a sexual hysteric of such a kind as in all periods is able to command allegiance; from him Wesley learnt much; and even his first sermon, based only on ex- perience of public speaking as an undergraduate, is said " to have driven fifteen persons mad." He later perfected his approach, and so many came to hear him that some had to swing like apes from the organ loft, " and altogether they made the church so hot with their breath that the steam fell from the pillars like drops of rain." The fields above Gloucester must often have heard the open-air sermons of Whitefield; during these performances strokes, convulsions, and self-maculation were common, and even sceptics were

so powerfully moved that one of them climbed a neighbouring
tree " and exposed his bare posteriors."

It was formerly usual for Gloucester to send every year
to the King a " lamprey pie, with raised crust " ; but this
was suspended at the accession of Queen Victoria, and not
even for the weathered palate of her successor was it to be
resumed.   Pins have been made here since 1626, and it was
long before then that the " monster bells " of a local foundry

[Drawn by W. H. Bartlett

134   THE NEW INN COURTYARD, GLOUCESTER, 1830

were celebrated.   This is a manufacturing town, and only its
capacious inns remain to show the economic structure of an
earlier age (134) ; its civic buildings are mostly good eighteenth
century—Gothic in St. Bartholomew's Hospital, Italian in
the Guildhall of 1749 ; the Infirmary (1755), and the County
Gaol (1784) are not, perhaps, on everybody's route, but with
Scheemaker's Snell monument in St. Mary de Crypt and the
sawn-off spire of St. Nicholas, with the lovely bronze knocker,
they are among the pleasant things of this uneven town.

Running up from Gloucester towards Worcester one is

naturally most aware of the water beside which the orchards
and the gigantic meadows are outstretched. There are such
willow-backed villages as Tirley, with its charming bridge
of 1825 ; at Ashleworth there is something of a quay ; even
if one strikes north one has still to cross the ferry at Twyning
(132). But even before one is out of Gloucestershire one
meets at Ashleworth the first of those enormous barns which
are the mark of Bredon country.

> " In summer-time on Bredon
> The bells they sound so clear ;
> Round both the shires they ring them
> In steeples far and near,
> A happy noise to hear."

Not a very good verse : one of those, perhaps, which
came with a little coaxing after lunch. But now that the bells
lie silent against a serious occasion, it is well to be reminded
how many lie close beneath this old hump, belying its former
lack of hospitality. (When digging was in progress at the
inner entrance to Bredon camp, several score of mutilated
heads, legs, and trunks were found.)

Bredon village itself has, besides the charming seventeenth-
century Giles Reed alms-houses, the very parent of all great
barns. This barn is 130 feet long and 40 feet in width,
divided into nave and aisles by the posts which support the
roof principals, and very suggestive of that interdependence of
sacred and profane building which is only now returning to
common practice, and of which there is a more practical
proof at Charlton, near Cropthorne, where the tithe barn has
been converted into a chapel-of-ease. These are fourteenth-
century barns, but at Crowle the barn is of the sixteenth, and at
Fladbury there is a smaller one from the fifteenth. Here and
at Middle Littleton the barns are not far from pigeon-cotes.

The slopes and purlieux of Bredon (135, 136) are an invitation to soft living, and know no industry more gross
than that of the silk-mills kept turning by a mill-stream at
Overbury. Overbury is a pretty got-up village on whose
upper slopes is laid out the estate of Overbury Court, a
charming piece of banker's prinking, in which the house
(younger than it is allowed to look) is surrounded by such
magnificent trees as those which Pliny's noble Roman used
to worship. Pastiches of this kind are common around
Bredon, and range from the vice-regal extravaganza of

R

Southam Delabere to the Roman imitation at Strensham Court. The last word in Anglo-Indian architecture (at Sezincote) is outside our boundaries, but meanwhile Southam Delabere will do well enough : at Strensham the enormous Grecian portico and overgrown estate have more charm than many authentic houses. Samuel Butler the earlier was born at Strensham, and some portraits painted by him were used to stop up the windows of a house at Croome ; happily, and although painters are usually good writers, writers are atrocious painters, and no one need regret these pictures. The general cosiness of houses in this mellow part is enhanced by a liberal use of stucco : this medium, recommended in 1736 as lightening the rooms, stopping the progress of fire, blocking dust, and making the whole house nearly soundproof, is readily abused ; but there is nothing to match it for economical elegance, and some houses round here (Wickhamford, for example) are almost East Anglian in the exuberance of their pargetting. Stucco is something very rare—an architectural medium which is perfectly elastic, raising no limit of size.

Bredon itself is easy to climb, and the view from its summit so remarkable that Fielding, never a great hand at describing scenery, withdrew entirely from the attempt, excusing himself on the grounds " first, we despair of making those who have seen this prospect admire our description ; secondly, we very much doubt whether those who have seen it would understand it." It is notorious, too, that those who have taken the trouble to climb to a point of vantage have invested already so much in the enterprise that expectation is monstrously inflamed ; let us therefore rather pursue the idea of Fielding into the town of Upton-on-Severn (37), in which Tom Jones fell out with a publican.

The " White Lion " still stands at Upton. Indeed, few towns can have more public-houses, and much time may be spent admiring the Palladian front of one, the convex brickwork of another, the stuffed fish in a third, and perhaps above all the beautiful position of the " Swan," so situated on the river bank that an observer standing to the west has a late Utrillo on his left, and an early Constable on his right. Upton is the Argenteuil of Birmingham, and on a summer Sunday in peace-time every kind of freshwater vessel appears on these fast-flowing stretches where to-day soldiers at exercise struggle against the current.

135   BREDON HILL FROM PENSHAM, IN BLOSSOM-TIME

136   A LANE NEAR BREDON VILLAGE

Upton is reached most conveniently by taking a car from
Pershore Station : the way there leads across Defford Common
and past the Folly of Dunstall Castle. This is in intention an
outrider of the Croome estate, but it is no longer visible from
there, and stands, with its phoney curtain wall, an obsolete
joke in this wilderness of brush and scrub. A wet afternoon
on Defford Common prepares us for the most recent association of Upton : for our area, which is not the Shakespeare
country only but also the George Eliot country, the D. H.
Lawrence and the Samuel Butler and some of the Savage
Landor country, has not long acquired its latest patron.
The Well of Loneliness begins at Upton, and it is these
early chapters which are the best of the book—so good,
indeed, that it is impossible to go about the most harmless
shopping in Upton without eyeing the formidable women
who stump on every side, in expectation of some fateful
meeting. Upton was also at one time the home of Dr. John
Dee, a Rosicrucian divine and astrologer, the first man to
lecture on Euclid in England. Elizabeth was a patron of
Dee, and magicians, as Frazer says, " constitute the oldest
professional class in the evolution of society." Dee, in the
final history of men, will come out higher than many of
those who, like Ursus d'Abitot, have left their names upon
the countryside.

Leaving Upton, it is the old church that is conspicuous,
the cupola upon the square Gothic sandstone tower (37) ; from
the train, and especially if the river is in flood, it might be
a town of the Low Countries, living off its cheese and the
great belted cattle for which Eastington, a mile or so from
Upton, is well known, depending for society upon the people
of the barges (and to-day the river patrol).

Assisi without St. Francis, Annecy without Rousseau, are
still enchanting places ; but Malvern (32, 115) without Mr.
Shaw is not very much. There is a lot of initial bluff-and
blow about it : the shelf-road is exciting ; the railway, cut
through orchards of plum and damson, agreeably soothing ;
even along the summit of the range, pursued by the paper-
chasers, the geologists, and the manly excitement of the boy-
scout game, there is a kind of windy distinction about the
town. But he would be wise who turned the other way and
went over into Herefordshire : here the whole pace and
temper of the scene are sensibly changed. East of the range

[*This and Figs. 138, 139 drawn by H. Inigo Triggs*
137   A DOVECOTE, ODDINGLEY

is one enormous plain, in which individual departures from the flat are scarce admitted by the eye (1, 32). But once over the top and past the British Camp, once within hail of that now rebuilt "mansion with minarets in the Eastern style" in which Elizabeth Barrett used to live, once at the summit of that road which could not wind more if it were the St. Gothard, there appears a rough, inflected landscape, full of surprise and, as it were, a warning of the Wales that lies on its western borders. Surprise in landscape is usually an element to which we ourselves contribute largely, but this part of Herefordshire, as if stung by the simplicity of the scene on the farther side of the Malverns, is said once to have taken itself the initiative. In 1575, on the word of a knight of the county, "Marcley Hill, after shaking and roaring for three days, to the great horror, fright, and astonishment of the neighbourhood, began to move at about 6 o'clock on Saturday evening, and continued walking till Monday at noon. It carried the

138   A DOVECOTE, DORMSTON

trees that grew on it, and the sheepcots and sheep grazing on it. It left a gaping distance 40 feet broad and 4 score ells long." This is an imaginative countryside, and richer in myth than its neighbour : at Mordiford church, some way beyond Much Marcle, there is the Mordiford dragon, a creature 12 feet in length, which formerly haunted the woods around the village, looting and savaging, until one day a condemned criminal was set to extinguish him. But if the area has legends such as this, to which an echo could be found perhaps in Kharkov, New England, or the Niger valley, it has also monuments immovable in space or time. At Mordiford itself the manor is of the eighteenth century ; but more splendid is the dovecote, itself of 1704 and thus one of the latest of these vernacular buildings. Ninety-three dovecotes have been counted in Worcestershire alone, and in Warwickshire there are some early prizes of this genre : that at Kinwarton dates from 1360, is 75 feet in circumference, and contains 600 nesting holes. The pigeon has always been a destructive, gluttonous bird, and only the Lord of the Manor and the Rector were allowed to put up these dovecotes (in France a similar *droit de colombier* was a source of irritation in 1789) ; mostly they were round, sometimes even 100 feet round, like the one at Great Hillborough, but there are also the octagonal brick-and-sandstone example at Wasperton, and the rectangular one at Wilmcote. Inside, surrounded by walls as thick as those of a castle, the returning birds were fed with a cake which could not, even in this third year of war, be the object of human envy. " Salt-cat " it was called, and into it there

139 A DOVECOTE, MUCH MARCLE

went mostly salt and cat, but also clay, to taste, and a handful of chopped meal : the whole was baked.

Most of us have had our fill of ruins, and the sight of gutted Stoke Edith is not the physical affront which it might have been four years ago. Yet this, like Holland House and the quadrangle of Gray's Inn, was a part of English living ; it had a big scheme, executed by Thornhill, and it had a witty and elaborate embroidered house and estate upon one of its

[Drawn by W. A. Forsyth, F.R.I.B.A.

140   LEDBURY MARKET HALL

walls (142). Country houses in general do not suffer from bombing : their fate is more often one of acquiescence, as they are made into warehouses or office blocks ; only a few stand idle, with shutters up in front and Mariana's blue fly singing on the scullery pane. Nesfield and Humphrey Repton have been to work on the estate of Stoke Edith ; but here nature has the better of the landscape gardener, for not far away an upcast of the upper Silurian rocks allows a view, not only of the luxuriance of Hereford, but of portions of

142 STOKE EDITH GARDENS IN THE LATE SEVENTEENTH
CENTURY, IN PETIT-POINT EMBROIDERY

141 THE LONG CANAL, WESTBURY COURT,
ON SEVERN

143   COVENTRY CATHEDRAL
AFTER THE FIRST RAID:
November 1940

thirteen other counties at once. Stoke Edith church, which
was mostly rebuilt in 1740 in the Grecian style, with Doric
columns and cornice, is a sitting target for philistinism.

Ledbury is a mostly black-and-white town (140), but on
one side of its main street there are many charming windows,
doors, and pieces of lettering that show the continuity of
trade which, until recently, made shopping in all market-
towns a personal pleasure. There are four major black-and-
white houses in Ledbury—Ledbury Park and the Talbot and
the Feathers hotels and the Court by the church—but there
are two very beautiful houses of a later period : one is called
Home End, and the other is the Police Station. Coming back
from Ledbury one passes at Eastnor an obelisk to the Hon.
Major E. C. Cocks, killed at Burgos in 1812 : this, ringing
like an unanswered telephone across a hundred and thirty
years, is the emblem of an earlier Spanish war than that in
which John Cornford and Julian Bell were killed, of one in
which Landor fought, while Byron, sailing up the Archipelago,
was suddenly aware of the battle for Madrid.

Worcester (38, 43) is best approached by road or train
from the Malverns : it is by the old Hereford road one passes
the wooden porch at Bransford, and by both one runs in
by that water-front and through those public gardens which
give Worcester a European air. By train it looks otherwise,
and from one's window it is the industry of Worcester, the
geometry of cranes and roofs and private railway systems,
that one sees first.

George III., on a visit to Worcester in 1788, had been
round the whole of the city, paid his devotions, and break-
fasted by seven o'clock in the morning ; modern visitors,
taking into account the development of the city, may not
decently be finished by half-past eight. A course about
Worcester is best plotted by the four Renaissance churches
which give the skyline an amenity unwonted in Midland
towns ; there is little black and white in Worcester excepting
Friar Street (43), and much of the later building is mean. A
lot of things are made in Worcester : " horse-hair and
damask," we read, " bricks and porcelain, carriages and
sauces and gloves," and then, with fine candour : " vinegar
and British champagne." These occupations have not made
Worcester beautiful, but they have given her a smell of
activity ; no one can walk along her peeling water-front, or

up the narrow hill-streets in which one church after another falls happily upon the eye, without recognising this as no idle town. In the High Street again, there is Thomas White's Guildhall, finished in 1712. This is a lovely fastidious red-and-yellow building, but impossible to photograph or even to see in proportion, so close, on the opposite side of the road, is the enclosed and covered market. This Guildhall, which contains a portrait of George III. by Reynolds, is a model of civic building, and shows in its ornament a monarchical bias very fitting in this last of all cities to surrender to the forces of Parliament. Not only are Charles I. and Charles and Anne set on the façade, but Cromwell is nailed by the ears above the door. The Deanery, of which the elevation was completed by Bishop Hough in 1723, and one or two houses in the Close, are eloquent of that good living and temperate thinking which are not only gracious in themselves but (as one may judge from the frequency with which men of great parts turn out to be the children of clerics) an augury for later generations. But once on profane ground the visitor might well regret an earlier, convertible Worcester —that, for instance, of 1575, which was " white-limed, and washed in comely colours " against a visit by the Queen ; and the Commandery, at least, remains from that time. This charitable house is one among many in this area which have been kept sweet by centuries of well-doing, and remain, with oriel and hammer-beam, refectory and staircase cut from a single oak, lovely and beneficent as ever. Many, that is, but not all : for within an hour's run from Worcester there are almshouses as old as this which were yet overthrown in a night and lay like sawdust men in the autumn drizzle.

It is difficult to say anything new of Coventry (34, 41) ; yet this was the first great sacrifice of our people, the first of our towns to take something of what has come to Rotterdam and Warsaw, to Belgrade and Kiev (113, 143). And Coventry was a worthy champion of our island. Those who stood with the Provost and his officials in Bailey Lane, those who, though elderly and unaided, climbed high upon the flaming roofs of the Cathedral, those who sheltered in the crypt and heard above them the whole countenance of this great fabric falling through itself—these knew that, as always in war, the best was being taken in surety for the whole. The cinemas stand, and the multiple stores and the villas, but not the four aisles, the pentagonal apse, and the chapels of the Drapers and the Girdlers, the Cappers and the Mercers, the Dyers and the Smiths (143); some of these guilds are still in existence, and used to use their original chapels for their assemblies. A winter and summer have passed over these ruins and those adjoining them; judgment is no longer given in St. Mary's Hall, and virtue no longer rewarded in the hospital; and the cathedral itself, with its tower and spire still reaching a hundred yards above the city centre, is still a sight to make one's eyeballs turn about. " It is astonishing to see what immense stones the heat had in a manner calcined, so that all the ornaments, columns, friezes, capitals, and projectures of many Portland stone flew off, even to the very roof, when a sheet of lead covering no less than six acres was totally melted : thus lay in ashes that most venerable Church, one of the most ancient pieces of piety in the Christian world." That is Evelyn on Old St. Paul's : but it may stand for Coventry, and for all places where the air is singed with the sudden denial of adoration.

At Warwick, there has been no such denial : time passes very evenly, knocking out a bow-window, peeling the stucco from the back of an inn, re-facing the piers of some substantial house set back a little from the road. The castle is very bold at a distance, and owes much to its situation, the river below, the elms beside, and the rooks above (78) ; but no period is less accessible to us than that of the builders of this barbican ; at table with Augustine, for example, or Charles V., or Alexander, many of us might put up a show, but the Renaissance, which came five generations late in England, is a barrier on the near side of which one is happy to find Sir Fulke Greville. This Greville, sprung from an old Campden wool-family and grandson of his namesake buried at Alcester, restored the whole fabric at the beginning of the seventeenth century, and it is from this time that its frankly decorative aspects are stressed.

Fulke Greville, a friend of Elizabeth and intimate adviser of James I. (who was four times a guest at Warwick), was a true man of the English Renaissance, of which his " I love God, and know the world," is indeed an excellent summary. Warwick has not many ancient buildings, for the fire of 1694 made short work of timber and clay. Mill Street and Leicester's Hospital (13) are exceptions in a town to which the

pretty Georgian bridge, the Jacobean Hospital of St. John,
the house in which Landor was born, and the 1780 Church
of St. Nicholas are the most reliable clues. It is about Warwick,
and particularly to south and east, that the park-like character
of this county is most evident. There is no prospect that is
not finite and domestic; one is rarely out of sight of the
roofs, the wood-smoke, or the clustering ornamented Tudor
chimneys which are the sign of people living in tame country
for warmth, or comfortable seclusion, or pleasure in one
another. The great parks of Charlecote and Packwood,
Rugby and Westwood, are not conspicuous in this landscape,
and their character is held even to the outskirts of Birmingham
to Hagley and Halesowen. Halesowen is now well engulfed,
and it was at the Lyttelton Arms at Hagley that Joseph
Chamberlain made his first political speech. But Birmingham
(as is clear from our illustration of St. Philip's (44)) was at
one time a model of late eighteenth-century planning, and
there are preserved at Aston Hall the panelling and mantelpiece from a house in Old Square. It was a great town for
books—for reading and writing, and printing and selling.
It was as the guest of a bookseller (lying, indeed, between a
bookseller's sheets) that Johnson, too idle to write, dictated
his first publication. The act of writing is itself a corrective;
and yet in this translation of Lobo's *Voyage to Abyssinia* there
is already something of the later excellence of Johnson's
prose. This was in 1733; in 1776, Johnson returned to
Birmingham with Boswell. Living much in the world of
ideas, he did not allow the expansion of the city to interrupt
his discourse on legitimation by subsequent marriage: but
Boswell not only ate with Quakers and magnates, but went
out to Soho, where the " vastness and contrivance " of the
machinery seemed to him to match those of Johnson's mind;
here also Mr. Bolton (whom Boswell contemplated as an
" *iron chieftain* ") made an early admission of the purpose of
Birmingham. " I sell here, sir," he said, " what all the world
desires to have—Power." How effectively this has continued
to be true may be judged from Dr. G. C. Allen's masterly
studies (themselves sponsored by one of the most successful
exponents of the maxim). In Johnson's time there had been
such new buildings as that of King Edward VI.'s Grammar
School (of 1707, replaced in 1832 by a design of Barry) or
the Bluecoat School of 1724. Best of all there was St. Philip's.

Vanbrugh was almost exclusively an architect in masses : every one of his works can be reduced to a series of triumphal arches, and Thomas Archer, his reputed pupil, has retained enough of this trait to make his church, which is not remarkable in detail, a vigorous, almost festive design. Few secular buildings of this period have been allowed to remain, and in their place are such experiments as the Doric Market Hall of 1833, Pugin's Roman Catholic Cathedral of 1839 (in which the pulpit is from Louvain, the stalls from Cologne) and the Town Hall by Hansom and Welch. Civic development reaches a new stage in Corporation Street, for which a special Birmingham Improvement Act was swept through Parliament by Joseph Chamberlain. Yet there were other elements in Birmingham : Burne-Jones left his mark in St. Martin's and St. Philip's : Newman was Superior of the Oratory of St. Philip Neri, an Italian building on the Hagley Road.

It is in this element of surprise that Birmingham, more than many less practical towns, is truly of Shakespeare's England. For there is no turn of this countryside at which nothing unexpected comes to view : even the ditches, the least assuming of all the elements of landscape, carry often within their depths that hemlock root by which the formidable heart of Socrates was made to cease ; the regular flatness of the Malvern plain is broken by such sudden bluffs as that on which is Hill End Court, oddly remote with its Georgian brick farmhouse and stone barns overlooking an islanded square mile of flat East Anglian grazing ; a mile or so from Cropthorne and the horreum area of Evesham are the hills around the Lenches, in which, after rain, the smallest breeze will bring the heavy scent of sodden foliage, the slightest unusual noise arouse a pheasant and send him beating and flapping higher up the range. Not far from Droitwich and in the centre of the park country there is just such a sandy, poplar-shaded, mushroom-smelling road as those over which one would rush to make a first-night halt at Rheims ; a little north is the valley of the Teme (122, 124–25), escaping, in the word of a geologist, " through a great fissure, and a point of extraordinary convulsion." This valley has such excitements as Rosebury Rock, on which the vegetation attains an almost tropical density, with ivy predominant, and the purple sandstone height of Old Stoorage Hill. At Knightwick there was an oak with mistletoe upon it.

Nor are its personal associations less regularly apt. Few figures in this war, for example, are more stirring than the guerrillas, the partisans who, whether in Esthonia or Albania, in Crete or the Pripet marshes, stubbornly contest their familiar ground ; and here at Woodbury Hill near Witley were once stationed the forces of Owen Glendower. These, with their French allies under Montmorency, were routed and pursued, but never cut to pieces, by Henry IV. and his son, the future hero of Agincourt. Retiring into their own ground, they fought a harrying defensive action for several years. At Thorngrove, in Worcestershire, there exists another parallel, expounded by Sir Charles Oman in a recent letter to *The Times* : for here Lucien Bonaparte was interned with his family between 1810 and 1814, and it is possible to see this as analogous to the détention of Rudolf Hess. Possible, but unjust, for this brother of Napoleon, who engineered the civil side of the Brumaire *coup d'état* and later, preferring the society of his wife and children to the honours of a principality, retired to Rome, was a most honourable, learned, and engaging figure. Unenvious of the dynasty, he brought up his son to be a botanist, and wrote himself a poem in many books on Charlemagne ; in fact, his English period was probably a happy one, for all that his voyage from Rome was for many years a favourite subject of *peintures de genre*, in which the exile was shown reading aloud from the dispatches of Jena, gazing fondly towards the coasts of France, and even, on one occasion, tatting.

No one is now able to travel very far for pleasure ; and no one, having travelled a little way, can remain for long a casual visitor. This book is meant to show that these brief, permitted journeys need not, none the less, be desultory, and that the smallest exploration of this middle and heart of England can remain a cell of excitement and inquiry in the mind, of refreshment and instruction in the senses. Long after we have been dragged through the orchards and over the rivers, under the hills and out of the Shakespeare country, there will persist above the alcaics of the train such a heart-breaking song as this of Ivor Gurney :

> Only the wanderer
> Knows England's graces,
> Or can anew see clear
> Familiar faces.
>
> And who loves joy as he
> That dwells in shadows ?
> Do not forget me quite,
> O Severn meadows.

INDEX

(The references in heavy type refer to the *figure numbers* of the illustrations)

149

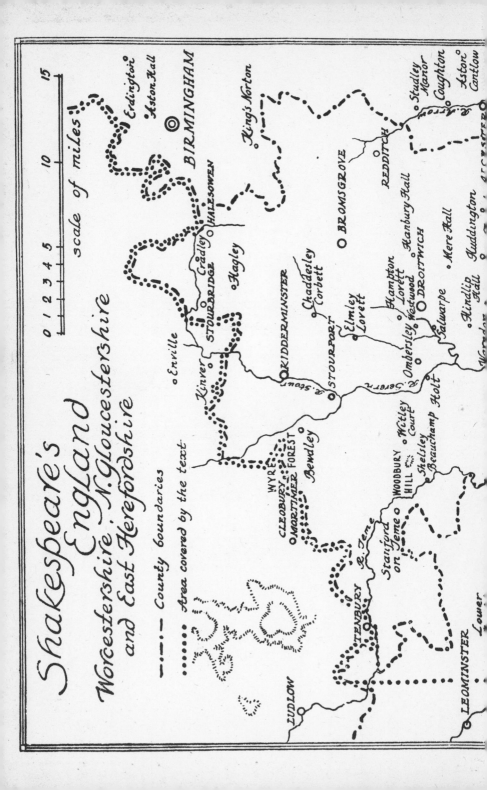

Shakespeare's England

Worcestershire, N. Gloucestershire and East Herefordshire

scale of miles

0 1 2 3 4 5   10   15

—·— County boundaries

•••••• Area covered by the text

Erdington°   °Aston Hall

◎ BIRMINGHAM

King's Norton

Studley Manor °
Coughton °
Aston ° Cantlow

○ BROMSGROVE

REDDITCH ○

Hanbury Hall
WORCESTER

Cradley
HALESOWEN

STOURBRIDGE
° Hagley

Chaddesley Corbett
KIDDERMINSTER

Enville

Kinver

R. Stour

STOURPORT

Elmley Lovett
Hampton Lovett
Ombersley
Westwood
DROITWICH
Salwarpe
° Mere Hall
° Hindlip
Hindlip Hall
Huddington
Warndon

R. Severn

Bewdley

WYRE
CLEOBURY
MORTIMER FOREST

WOODBURY HILL
Shelsley
Beauchamp
Witley Court
Holt

Stanford on Teme

R. Teme

TENBURY

LUDLOW

LEOMINSTER
Lower